LOVE, KURT

Love, Kurt

The
VONNEGUT LOVE LETTERS,
1941–1945

KURT VONNEGUT, Jr.

EDITED BY

EDITH VONNEGUT

RANDOM HOUSE

NEW YORK

Published in the United States by Random House,
an imprint and division of Penguin Random House LLC, New York.

RANDOM HOUSE and the HOUSE colophon are
registered trademarks of Penguin Random House LLC.

Hardback ISBN 978-0-593-13301-9
Ebook ISBN 978-0-593-13302-6

Printed in China on acid-free paper

randomhousebooks.com

2 4 6 8 9 7 5 3 1

First Edition

Book design by Barbara M. Bachman

CONTENTS

I FOUND THESE LETTERS WRITTEN FROM MY FATHER, Kurt Vonnegut, to my mother, Jane Marie Cox, deep under the eaves of the attic in the big old house where I grew up, buried beneath fifty-five years of the flotsam and jetsam that our mother would not or could not throw away. Every report card, every cocktail napkin, every Christmas card ever received was there. A single ice-skate guard; broken reel-to-reel tape players; moldy sleeping bags; mess kits; stacks of vinyl records; Sears, Roebuck catalogs from the 1950s. On the very bottom of these strata was a squashed white gift box sealed with brittle yellowed tape.

Over the years, the attic's contents had been dripped on from a leaking roof, gnawed on by mice, and sprinkled with acorns from squirrels that had somehow gained entry. Draped on top of everything were slabs of pink cotton candy–like insulation that had fallen down from between the rafters. I'd seen plenty of places like this while foraging at estate sales, but never so dense and familiar. Our mother had a certain sense of tidy order, but zero editing skills. She thought everything mattered or would eventually. Any organization she'd hoped to keep was destroyed by us kids regularly tossing it all like a salad when looking for something, or stuffing additional items in there for safekeeping. An undiscerning eye would have scanned the sodden pile and chucked the whole lot.

But while my mother was a natural hoarder, I am a natural scavenger.

Yard sales and dumps are my playground. Always sifting deeper than most, looking for treasure, I have no end of patience for going through piles of apparently worthless stuff. I am a connoisseur of junk, ever searching for the rare and precious. I see now that I was in training to find the most precious treasure of all.

There in the attic, as the archaeologist in me excavated below decades of family accumulation, I found the Lucy of Dad. The earliest inklings of who he was going to become. The first sparks that lit the dazzling Roman candle that was my father. Two hundred and twenty-six letters that he wrote to my mother from 1941, when he was just nineteen years old, to 1945, when he was twenty-four.

Some are typed, using the typewriter as an artistic tool the way a painter uses a brush, and some are handwritten and illustrated in pencil. His penmanship is remarkably legible, and as with the content of his novels, you never have to struggle to decipher what he is saying. These letters show that my father was well formed as a writer at a strikingly young age. He just lacked confidence, an audience, and experience. My mother became his confidante and audience before he dared to even refer to himself as a writer. The experience would come soon enough.

Kurt pursued Jane for four years with these astonishing letters. It is thrilling to read how in love with her he was. She was the single object of his desire. He half-heartedly dated other women and would say they had the right body but the wrong soul. My father's intense love for my mother, expressed in his crystal-clear handwriting, is breathtaking—and also devastating, knowing what I know now: that he would stop loving her. Would Romeo have left Juliet eventually if they had lived long enough? How could a love so dazzling and singular and determined fizzle?

When I went up to the attic that day, I was not expecting to find more than some old bank statements. The discovery floored me figuratively and literally. I spent the next four hours with the box between my legs, reading letters written seventy-seven years ago. Knowing full well how it all turned out made for a powerful emotional cocktail. My heart broke for my mother and father. I don't cry very often, but I had to be careful handling the fragile papers as tears slid down my cheeks.

THIS COLLECTION IS A PORTRAIT of first love and early ambition, and what was found and born and lost between two brilliant young minds and hearts. If I had been my mother when he was leaving twenty-five years later, I would have dug out those letters and thrown them in his face, yelling "What about these!? See how relentlessly you pursued me? You vowed we'd grow old together, love each other forever, and do so much good in this life. What about those promises, you asshole?!!" But my mother wasn't like that.

Their marriage did not survive, but the letters did. In my estimation they are among his finest writing, right up there with *The Sirens of Titan, Cat's Cradle,* and *Slaughterhouse-Five.* They come from a time and place more passionate, pure, and inspired than any other in his life. He was not writing for fame or money, but to win the love of a woman.

LOVE, KURT

PRE-1941:
TWO INDIANAPOLIS FAMILIES

KURT'S PARENTS WERE GERMAN AMERICAN, SECULAR humanists. His mother, Edith Lieber Vonnegut, was born to a wealthy beer-brewing family in Indianapolis. The brewery suffered a catastrophic downturn during Prohibition, and the Great Depression further eroded their fortune. Kurt's father, Kurt Vonnegut, Sr., was the son of the first licensed architect in Indiana and an architect himself. Kurt junior was the youngest of three children, five years younger than his sister, Alice (Allie), and eight years younger than his brother, Bernard. He was the doted-upon baby of the family and enjoyed a loving, lively childhood.

Jane was from a Quaker family of Anglo-Irish descent. Her father, Thomas Harvey Cox, was an Indianapolis lawyer. Her mother, Riah Fagan Cox, held a master's degree in classical literature; she coauthored a grammar textbook that would go on to become a standard in the field. She also taught at the Orchard School, the primary school that both Kurt and Jane attended. Up until Jane left for college, her life was dominated by the unpredictable health of her brother and mother. Riah was a brilliant scholar and teacher, but she suffered from episodes of mental collapse for which she was periodically institutionalized. Jane's only sibling, Gussie, was mentally fragile as well, after a surgical accident severed a facial nerve, leaving his face slightly disfigured.

1941:
FIRST LOVE

KURT AND JANE ATTENDED SCHOOL TOGETHER FROM KINdergarten through third grade at the Orchard School in Indianapolis, but they didn't encounter each other again until they were nineteen, when they both attended a social at the local Woodstock Country Club on August 15, 1941. They discovered they shared a passion for social justice, an altruistic desire to contribute to the world, and a love for art in all its forms. They formed a deep bond that evening and spent almost every minute together for the next ten days, until he left for Cornell University and she for Swarthmore College for their sophomore years. This is when their correspondence began. (My mother's nickname was Woofy, as you'll see in the letters. I have no idea why. I don't think she liked it, because it was never used after college, and when I asked, I never got a satisfying answer.)

Jane was an excellent student. Having always loved books, she majored in literature, with minors in philosophy and history. A former boyfriend once described her as an "extraordinarily cute, lovely young lady with a challenging intellect."

Kurt, meanwhile, was *not* a good student. He was poorly matched to his major: chemistry. His father and brother felt strongly that science was the future and had urged young Kurt to study that field. In reality, he spent most of his time editing Cornell's newspaper, *The Daily Sun,* and writing to Jane. He was almost singularly focused on her and became frustrated when she did not write more often. Jane, on the other hand, was enjoying a heavy course load and many suitors, as she was enchanting, beautiful, smart, and away from an unhappy home for the first time. Her freedom had just begun. She must have been hesitant to allow Kurt to tie her down so quickly, even though he was already asking her to marry him in his earliest writings to her. His devotion to her was unusual for the time; the norm in the 1940s was for young men and women to date a variety of people. I don't think Jane was expecting Kurt to become so exclusively enamored with her after their summer romance. That they were in different states and different schools made total commitment extra-impractical.

On December 7, 1941, Pearl Harbor was attacked, leading President Franklin D. Roosevelt to ask Congress to declare war on Japan. America entered World War II.

Dear Woofy, darling, sugarfoot, sweet, angelface:

I'm writing this letter on Thursday night,
September 18, 1941, listening to the Maxwell House
radio program at its mid-point. With dogged depend-
ibility that radio program will end, ~~the~~ you will
open this letter ~~xxxxxxxxx~~ after the passage of
another number of seconds, and with the same surity,
the time will come when we will be living and loving
together for the ~~greatest~~ part of our lives. I
                greater
just watched a minute pass; do the same, darling,
and kiss the clock. We're winning, can't you see,
we're winning!!!

House party--I'll lose my shirt for the first
time--will be about November first. You sexy little
love affair for a lifetime, I'm coming down to see
my wife about October 16, 17, 18. I'll expect to
get off the train and into your cool arms to feel
your young restless body against mine. Come
naked to the waist, I'll do the same--what am I
saying? I hope Pennsylvania is as nice about beer
as New York. Will the corn belt ever learn? I'll
be broke, darling--love, love, love...I'll continue--
and I shan't be able to support you in the manner I'd
like you to be accustomed to. Please don't fall in
love with a Princeton hacker with a billfold. Love
good old me; sleep on that, will you? Say to yourself
ten times a day, "I love wonderful, wonderful, oh so

peachy Kurt, and if I don't marry ~~him~~ the guy he'll
kill me--and he will too."   You might add that I've
got a gun and haven't missed since the age of eight.
~~Tell that to some of the boys.~~

I'm crazy to get to work...I've had the moaning
blues for four nights in a row. Kissing a locket and
talking to a stuffed ~~xxxii~~ yellow duck wearing an im-
ported Scandanavian necktie fall short, way short. I
don't like learning from life.

~~XXXXXXXXXXXXXXXXXXXXXXXXXXXXXXXXXXXXXXXXXXXXX~~
~~XXXXXXXXXXXXXXXXXXXXX~~

Your letter was an oasis, darling, and it doesn't
~~take sand to make a desert.~~   It takes sand to make
an hour glass, and that's what's clogging our lives.

I love you, darling--those four words are all
yours.   That leaves me six words in any telegram.
I don't think I'll use them.

This letter is marked like a piece of sun copy--
Thoreau would ~~xxxx~~ approve; it's practical.

I lahof you.

KURT

I KISSED
IT. KISS
IT, DE-
TACH AND
RETURN,

8

--Now the whole of Cornell knows about it. I've laid
a bet with a brother from Philadelphia that I'll marry
you in eight years--$50.   And for every year before
that that I am married to you I get, we get, a bonus of
$10+++++!

Do you realize how long we can live on that sort of
money, just getting out of bed for meals?

I love you, and did you know that you have thirty-
five trillion (35,000,000,000,000) red corpuscles in
your shapely body, and that laid edge to edge they would
extend around the world about three times at the equator?

What did I say that you tried to shock your room-mate
with? --I completely forget.   Should I tone down? Sex
is a real part of everyone's life--sex is peachy.   Why
bury it with things low and vulgar.   It's wonderful, and
the most dynamic experience that will ever warp my life
about itself.

I love you.

Kurt Vonnegut — Jr.

he enclosed gadget will hold up in any court, ammounting
to a public declaration of intentions.   If I don't marry
you in '45, sue me--I'll have it coming to me plus a lot of
misery.

Hope the symbolism is clear. We'll put it on
our first station wagon.   I love you; not
more than life itself, because you are life.

Dearest Woofy:

I was just thinking about your fourth dimension — the dimension in which you are Jane Marie Cox, not simply Jane Cox. How much prettier Jane Marie is than Jane. I love Jane but I'm terribly in love with Jane Marie. I just met her a couple of weeks ago and yet I'm sure that I could be happy with her for a lifetime.

Jane Marie is the entirely fascinating woman you promise to be — the depth and emotion and fullness which are all yours. Mr. Butler used to tell Samuel that he respected old Mr. Pontifex, not because he had done anything particularly wonderful, but because he was sure that should a need, any need, for such an act ever present itself, Mr. Pontifex would surely be able to handle it.

—KURT

115

Dear Woofy:

I've got a brilliant start on my novel...torn up
the first chapter and a half.   If you inspire me,
and I know damned well you can, I'll write one about
you.   Lovingme is a prerequisite, however.   Do you?
I do.

The spacer on the typewriter is broken.   I've
rigged up a neat little gadget, Mr. Failey's pipe and
two rubber bands, whichworks beautifully (except between the words loving and me and which and works).   If
it becomes standard equipment on Royal Typewriters I'll
retire and marry you in a week.

I keep wanting to kiss you which is damned hard
to do from ~~the~~ four-hundred miles away.   Skip's
getting ~~xxxxx~~ sick of my getting up in my sleep and
kissing him.   He's notvery good at it.   You are.

I got in a ~~pol~~ political argument with Nancy,
defending Britain, and Skip, Bob, Mrs. Failey, her
brother, Mr. Failey, the cook, and myself damning her.
I tried to pump her for information about you...claimed
she knew nothing.

I love you first, Alice next, mother next, Mary Jo
next, followed by a raft of insignificant creatures
struggling for recognition.

XXXx.

KURT

SAVE ME 90%
OF ALL DATES
BETWEEN SEPT.
1-11. THE 11TH
IS IMPORTANT.

XXX GODDAM POSTOFFICE PEN

Marry me in
1945 ———

This one cost 15¢

Beyond the turn where the
roadway winds
Through the mist of far away
The sun still shines its
rays of hope
Behind the clouds of gray;
And through the misty shadows
Where the light seems lost from view
The thoughts of those who understand
Remain to comfort you.

Love
Kurt

X X X X X X X X X

13

Dearest Jane—

This is a prelude to Physics, eight minutes away. Laws affecting bodies in motion are the current concern of the course, fitting handily into my mental state. —Incidentally, I think I'm doing damned well without a typewriter, a phenomenon which here-to-for you've never observed. Entirely legible, I think — let me know if there are any doubts in your mind (admirable gadget) as to the nature of the characters.

Writing columns (bless you, sweet child, for seeing their merits) is usually forbidden to sophomores, and the concentration of my work is bound to become more and more dilute. However, I've been writing anonymous sports stories every day, describing the adroit functionings of the freshman football team, and more recently, cross country. I love you.

In Physiology now — miserable course because of the instructor. I haven't got a prayer of a decent grade — too damned bored. It has its practical applications — I'll listen. I'm feeling damned blasé about school in general. It's a lapse, due to develop into a windsprint beginning this afternoon, Monday, lasting past prelims next week, followed by absolutely extra-curricular activities involving yourself.

We gave one helluva good beer party for the freshmen. Your hubby succeeded in being entirely blotto — the pleasant way. I lost my voice for the whole week-end.

We're going to build a new bar right after fall house party. We've got a crumby but entirely functional one now. It'll be completed in time for Junior Week, sometime in February, to which I now invite you. ——— darling.

Do you mind if I spend a great deal of my Thanksgiving vacation with you? — beginning about November 22. I love you.

DAMMIT! YOU'VE GOT TO COME HERE AS EARLY ON FRIDAY, OCTOBER 31ST, AS YOU POSSIBLY CAN. THERE'S A TRAIN THAT PULLS OUT OF HERE FOR PHILLY ABOUT MIDNIGHT SUNDAY. I'LL BUY YOU A BERTH IF YOU'LL STAY TILL THEN. —— ONE WORD FROM YOU AND I'LL SHARE IT.

I love you.

KURT

THE WORKS OF

Henry D. Thoreau

WITH A BIOGRAPHICAL SKETCH BY

Ralph Waldo Emerson

Thomas Y. Crowell Company

NEW YORK: 1940

.O JANE — WHOM I LOVE
AND SHALL LOVE ALL MY
LIFE. — TO BE SHOWN TO
OUR CHILDREN WHEN THEY
BEGIN TO WONDER WHAT
THINGS ARE MOST IMPORTANT
IN THIS WORLD THAT SOME
FOOLS CALL HELL.

   - PRESENTED WHEN WE
WERE TOO YOUNG TO EVEN
BE ENGAGED.

(KURT)

9/14/41

Dearest Jane, Snow White...

Tonight I ~~am~~ am a stooge, something I will never tolerate in later life--I've got too many chromosomes. About us you see the rather nifty offices of the Cornell Daily Sun. I'll kiss you in them on Novexmber first, an event without precedent, I'm sure. I'm writing headlines; being told by another person just how long they must be, and what they must say. Oh dammit! Abraham Lincoln, J. Christ, Mickey Mouse, or Freud never took orders ~~frams~~ from anybody in later life--later life again, these are thought chains, darling, not classic literature.

You're mother's little testimonial made me feel as solid with the Coxes as Thoreau with a woodchuck. Rod Gould, cream on the mother's milk of DU described the document as facile and fluid. It set the house on its ear; they all want her up for houseparty.

I've designed a house, ~~xxx~~ plans for which will be neatly drawn up and mailed in due time. There's that word, our little chum that stuffs sand through hour glasses. My cold is gone and I'm raising hell in all my courses, and after rushing is over I'll knock the wind out of the goddam Sun. I haven't done a decent job on anything since Christ was a corporal, but with two mouths to feed a real machine hits the road next ~~Mxndxy~~ Monday.

You've given me a million ideas and a drive I've never had before, but my God I've got to see you, simply got to. I want a boost from you that'll set this foolish world of
                  and
inferior matings ~~x~~/chromosome atrocities on its bruised

fanny.

I'll be there the fifteenth or sixteenth, wearing a beat up sports coat, saddle shoes with paint from the bar all over them, torn flannel slacks with acid holes in them, not a cent in my pockets, clean underwear, sox, shirt and tie. Hide me from the boys, sugarfoot, but be nice to me, for God's sake love me; I'll have enough for an evening of brews and one for bruises.

I'll show you my text books--sexy, eh?--when you get up here. Damned if I want won't know plenty about plenty that people will pay me for. How much are babies? I love you.

Sorry, can't afford lingerie. You'll just have to go naked for the first few years. That's the way it'll have to be darling. I don't like the idea any more than you do, but we'll have a few lean years, and we wont always be lean.

Dearest Jane--stinky, darling:

Looking at our love from an abstract point of view--
I feel abstract this evening--we've gone through a psycho-
logical metamorphasis.   During our first biological en-
counters, remember? --it scared hell out of both of us; we'd
go home worried and bothered as hell. We weren't sure if
it was right--firx right? The most wonderful time was the
last one.   We were sure we were in love, probably for the
rest of a heavenly lifetime--darling, we laughed and made
love for the first time. That's the way it should be, that's
the way it will be--the one thing I live for, subconsciously,
is making love to you, laughing with you, having children
by you.   Damned if we haven't got the chromosomes!

As for the love vitamin, vitamin E is as close as they've
come to it.   It is known as the sterility vitamin; little
animals that don't get it in their diet--what a filthy trick,
even in a laboratory--lose their ability to reproduce and
their sexual characteristics.   Get loxts of whole wheat,
corn, and eggs,darling--I want a sexy wife.

Buck Young finally arrived.   The room looks quite
homey now--he brought several shot-glasses for our venition
glass collection.   We spent the day discussing our respective
wives and building a huge bookcase.   It's a darb.   If we
can afford a workshop in the basement, the studio comes first,
of course, I'd like to have one. Please?   Buck knows Fritzie
Gebhart at Swarthmore. We may be down to Philly for the
Cornell-Penn game on November 22.   This is tentative at
present, but God knows I want to take you--I think he likes
me a little.

I'm hacking at the Sun again. They may let me have a

column again.   I'm no newspaper man when it comes to writing
in plain English--I can't write in plain English--what Egor
Blotz said before the Cornell Society for the Exploration of
Physical Phenomena, or trudging up to the football field on
bleak November afternoons, every afternoon, to tease a story
on the freshman football team.   Helluva sentence--sorry I
started it.   Incidentally, you lovely little girl who loves
to be kissed on every inch of your fourteen square feet of
creamy skin--I'll do it too--you are the fortunate recipient
of a year's subscription to the Cornell Daily Sun. Delivery
begins with the first issue, Mondays, to be delivered to
you at Swarthmore. Oh, lucky you! Look for me on the editorial
page.

Damned if I'm not a better person since we've been in
love.   If you think you'll ever get that seven-eighths of
you that's in Ithaca back you're crazy. Why don't you come up
and live with me.   That's one helluva potent eighth you're
holding back, ix I want a complete set, the works, understand?
I'll have none of this short term loan foolishness.

When we're married we can economize on shirts. I swear
I'll never wear one with you under the same roof. I love you
more than a hacker can show on yellow paper with a grade B
typewriter.   My fingers wander idly over the noisey keys.
~~Ifxhxneverxfindxthexlostxchord~~ I'm still looking for the lost
chord. Untill then you'll have to be satisfied with Chopsticks.
I love you.

Kurt

CORNELL

MEN DON'T WEAR LIPSTICK, WELL, FOR MOST OF THEM ANYWAY-- GOD'S SAKE,

_21_

Dear Jane, Darling:

Everybody seems to know that I can do fourth year French, Qualitative Analysis, Histology, Physiology and Physics but me. I need a shot in the arm, which is figurtive, as I would hate to stuff you into a hypodermic syringe.

I'm coming to Swarthmore on the eighteenth in answer to clearly audible frustrated beatings on a voluptuous breast and outspoken demands from an excited endocrine system (them's glands).q We've been translating our love into sex, demands for which have been kicking hell out of us. We've got a damned site more than just that between us. That's what I really want to see in two weeks--I swear it; so help me, Zoroaster, I mean it.

I love you. Write me pretty quick.

I looked at part of you under a microscope today--damned instructive. It was a slice of Kurt Vonnegut, Jr. about two weeks before we get married...half of him. --Good looking little egg, literally and figurtively.

Don't be a psychologist unless you really want to. What about your being an English major? Don't ignore the chromosomes your mother handed down!

Dear Mrs. Cox

Your lovely daughter and myself have been invited to visit
the Bolgianos for Thanksgiving; very wonderful people, middle
aged parents of a fraternity brother of mine. Mrs. Bolgiano
will write you. On Wednesday, November 19th, Ralph Bolgiano
and myself are to pick up Jane at Swarthmore, and drive to his
Baltimore home. We are tentatively going to a formal dance
at Annapolis that night, as our part in National Defense. On
Thursday we shall have dinner with the family, sailing in the
afternoon. That evening, Jane and myself will be back at
Swarthmore, and I shall be dead-weight until Saturday. On
the afternoon of that eventful day, Cornell will challenge the
unbeaten might of Pennsylvania, a classic for which I have
choice tickets. I believe that there is a Swarthmore formal
that night.

I hope Jane's health wasn't harmed as a result of house-
party--she was, incidentally, the belle. In the course of
juvenile events there comes a time when one is likely to run
unintentionally afoul of parents. I have insinuated myself
into the lives of the Cox family. A parallel situation ex-
ists at the Vonnegut household through the vigorous efforts
of another anxious male. The family resents him furiously
with the exception of one supporter, Alice. I hope I have
the good will of the Coxes, and that there are few epithets
muttered at my frequent arrivals.

Jane and I are not going to be married in the next five
years, and we've got sound enough minds to know what we want
and to steer a straight course. --A statement that would
put worried parents happily to sleep all over the world.

Typing this sort of note ammounts to a fierce faux pas.
I am, however, absolutely helpless with a pen, having trans-
fered from Orchard School to public school during my form-
ative years.

Kurt Vonnegut--

1942:
JUNIOR YEAR

IN MAY 1942, CORNELL INFORMED KURT THAT IF THERE was no improvement in his grades, he would not be continuing at the university. He was failing biochemistry and organic chemistry and had been put on academic probation. Despite this, he ignored his junior year classes and channeled all his time into editing the *Sun* and writing to Jane. They continued to visit each other for parties and events at their respective campuses. (Most of the parties were at Cornell; Swarthmore was more of a buttoned-up institution.)

By December, Kurt was flunking out. He developed a mild pneumonia while home on Christmas break. Meanwhile, Jane was on course to having a stellar academic year, wholly focused on her studies. She didn't correspond with Kurt as often as he would have liked. All the while, the shadow of the war was looming closer to their lives.

Dearest Woof:

Remember our friends Yin and Yan?   A pleasing little circle made up of a pair of droplets, chinese symbols of man and woman, life. Look, where Yan is more narrow Yin is her fullest; and where Yin is weak Yan is his strongest. You see, darling, they fit neatly into the pattern like a jig-saw puzzle, not like bricks.

I swear before the maker of sycamores and little fishes that I adore you for being the heavenly cluster of ideas and woman you are. I would do anything on God's charred acre to make you happy. It may be poor technique, but I'm the truest bum you've ever come across.

As I left, you said that everything was all right again-- did you mean it? One century ago we agreed that our love was the most wonderful thing that had ever happened to either of us, and that we had to keep it alive. I still think so. Remember the ideas we shared? --our wish to cure an ailing world, our admiration for Thoreau, and our determination to pursue those things which are really important in life? --our house with a courtyard and a thick squat oak in its center? --our hacker's studio behind the house, our well-stocked bar? --our being called by name by every bar-tender in town? --our children with a brilliant heritage and healthy as hell? --our ambition to write great books, our plans to live in Europe for a while as news correspondents? --our disdain for stuffed shirts, our admiration for clever and creative friends? --our house full of dogs and bedroom full of bed? --our hearts full of love? Remember any of that?

Please write soon, darling---

(KURT)

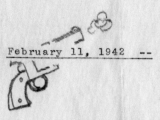

February 11, 1942 --

<u>Dearest Woofy:</u>

I'm really sorry about house-party because you had such
a miserable time. Little tales continue to come back to me
now, and I've said some things I certainly don't mean. Ralph
was a honey to take care of you as he did, and I've always
thought he was a helluva good egg. I'm not at all sure what
I said to you about yourself. There's not a damned thing about
you that I don't like. We simply don't belong together any more
than nitric acid and glycerine. There's the simple statement of
how I feel about the whole thing. You're a plenty wonderful
girl with a good mind. In that mind you have all the elements
of happiness: accomplishment and an appreciation of beauty.

In defense of my way of thinking, and my admiration for
the sciences: Through the history of mankind, this question
has been asked--"Why are we here, and what makes us act as
we do?" Religion after religion has formed in a fruitless
attempt to find some answer. I read the Gestalt theory five
minutes ago, and I can't see any application to my way of thinking. The proton, neutron, and electron are closer to an answer
to the question of life than any other offered. Science is broad,
not narrow, as so many persons smugly believe. When I first
fell in love with you, one electron hit another in my head, causing a chemical reaction, billions of electrons hitting billions
of other electrons. These electrons flowed through a conductor,
thexnerve a nerve, to all over my body, causing further reactions
wherever they flowed. Valves opened and closed; new chemicals
were poured into my bloodstream. I put my arm around you, kissed
you, told you I loved you. That one electron liked you better
than anybody else.

Now I'm being facetious, and I didn't mean to be. Love can't
be traced to a single electron, but things microscopic have certainly presented a clearer picture of man as a whole than he has
ever known before.

You've really had enough happiness? --the foolish game has
just started for us. My happiest moments are ahead of me. Do
I impress you as having lead a pretty unhappy life so far? Thanks
for your generous wish--I appreciate it, and should like you to
have the same. I see no reason why either of us should have a
very wretched time of it; unless we married each other.

This thing we used to have is no blot on my integrety, dammit!
Watch that sort of talk. I reserve all rights, as you do, to as
confused a state of mind as I damned please. I over-did this honesty business. Anything I felt like saying I said.

If you feel like writing as much as you say you do (honesty)
I wish you would.

Blue slipper
for my drill
coat.

Kurt - Jr.

VALENTINE GREETING *by* WESTERN UNION

721

P12- FT ITHACA N Y

JANE COX
SWARTHMORE COLLEGE
SWARTHMORE PENNA

YOU'RE LOVELY AND SWEET, A TREASURE DIVINE. YOU'RE ALL I WANT FOR

MY VALENTINE.

            TARZAN

Dear dear....

Kisses go "phfffffff."   I feel sexy as all hell.
I want to be a bad bad boy with the right person. Want to
be a bad bad, absolutely filthy little girl with me?

What a shot in the arm your letter beginning "Puddin'
dear--" was.   I needed it. I was up until three a.m. with
the Sun two nights ago, have been up past one a.m. in rush
meetings every other night, and have been xxxxxxxy severely
frightened in French, Physics, Histology, Qualitative analysis, and Physiology.   I wish you'd come up here and take
care of me.   I've got a bitch of a xix cold, and a physical
lust for you that has me walking on my heels. Love is physical, darling--we've got plenty of that plus an admiration
for each other, and a wonderful mental compatibility. What
else is there to marraige?   Go on, try and find a loop-hole.
Tell everybody that we're getting married...I'm no fool. I
know when I'm well off.

Here's an interesting biochemical-psychological point
which you can work on: despite the fact that I'm tired
and xxxx foghound by a cold, I still feel sexy, plenty sexy
--moreso than I have all week.   I'll expect a full report.

Theory on the Northern Lights, current: from time to
time, spots appear on the Sun, caused by masses of material
that are cooler than the rest.   These masses send out
streams of electrical particals, electrons, which move with
the speed of light, and which are quite invisible under the
most powerful microscopes--the smallest partical yet discovered. Some of these bits are attracted to the positive
North Pole.   They are then deflected back into the

stratosphere and back into space, appearing in the North
as light.

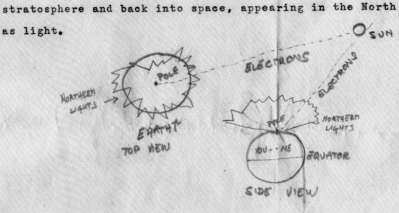

        ---See?

    Phffffffffff.   Phffffffffff. Pant. Phffffff.
My Gawd!   Phffffffffffffffffffffffff-phffff-phffffffffff.
    I have very little hair, darling, very little.   It may
be back by November first.   As a matter of fact, what there
is of it is very pretty. We've been painting the bar in prep-
aration of for you, and I got a quantity of white paint all
over me.

    I love you.   My regards to the family, play me up,
ease their minds, don't let them worry.   Don't let me
worry. I love you.

               KURT

My sox are size 11

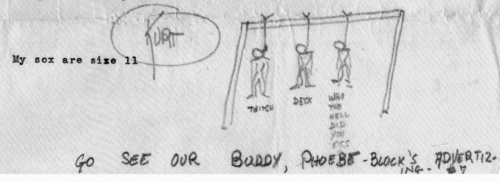

GO SEE OUR BUDDY, PHOEBE-BLOCK'S ADVERTIZ-
ING-BY

To Woofy, without whose inspiration this work would not have been
    possible--Kurt Vonnegut, Jr., July, 1942.

After serious meditation
I conclude that this vacation
Is a complex and very puzzling one.

It takes a mess of speculation
To foresee a deviation
From the circumstance which makes my efforts feeble.
Should we take to constant boating,
Spending fortunes while we're floating
On the sewage of four-hundred thousand people?

Tell me dear, where is this bower,
Built by God for youth in flower,
Whence we might pass the time without restraint?
If such a place lies in your knowledge,
Tell me ere I return to college
That I may rectify your often-voiced complaint.

The interior of a tan sedan
Cannot be part of nature's plan;
Brake and throttle, wheel and clutch strangle, rip, and smother.
For the sports of Aphrodite
I should prefer you in a nighty,
In a house without the presence of your parents or your brother.

Dear Love of my Life:

    I find these times trying and tiring--the three phases of
a befuddled life--you, studies, and the Sun.   I've received
beatings in each of these fields, and am now searching for an
ally.   John Barley-corn sorely betrayed me in that role Saturday night.

    However, the new me, recently completed, will enter into
the next semester smiling and confident.   Goals: to have you
completely convinced that none but my own nifty person could ever
keep you happy for a life-time; that, through my intensified
interest in studies I shall be able to keep you in voluptuous
comfort as my wife; and through becoming managing editor of the
Sun I'll prove to myself that I can do at least one thing god-
damned well.

    Please note that this childish sketch of my immediate ambit-
ions balances on a single, unstable fulcrum--you.   Because of
you I am ambitious and confident.

    Junior Week houseparty will be a toss of a coin for me--
double or nothing.   Out of 365 days the generous school fathers
have given me 20 for vacation.   My dish-washing job will pay
for my summer tuition (a scholarship!!).   I shan't see you after houseparty for months--almost a year.   I've got to convince
you to love me, keep on loving me, and live for the day we're
married.   That makes me a pretty conceited ass, but a pretty
determined one.   The simple fact is that I can't get along without you; not even now.
_____
    One hot, mid-western summer, two people met, a boy and a
girl.   After a dozen surprising days they realized that they
were in love, and each saw in the other something which they
had believed peculiar to themselves: imagination; imagination
and ideals.   Their imaginations ranged free and mingled, and
explored the fascinating length and breadth of a thousand dreams
and thoughts.   Where one was lost the other would lead the way.
They swore they had love, and were resolved to keep it.

    Seven years later, on another hot, midwester summer, a
troop train pulled into the smokey city--Japan was in ruins,
and the victorious dough-boys were back to learn the arts of
peace.   Lost in a sea of khaki, a lone sailor was swept bxxthe
along by a tide of men, rushing to kiss their wives and sweet-
hearts.   A little wearily, he shuffled down the dirty station
steps.

    A small voice called out his name.   In another second he
was kissing a girl: same boy, same girl, ideals, imagination,
mid-west.

    "Darling, I'll always love you," he whispered, and she new
he meant it--he'd never managed to say it quite that way before.
                    +   +   +
    ...No moral: same story, poorly told this time.

32

Dear Woofy:

The Indianapolis Wellesley Club has invited me to their
Back-To-School Dance at the Woodstock Club, Friday Evening,
September Fifth, Nine to One. Please go with me.   I'll
browbeat somebody up here into teaching me to jitterbug--
Oh damn but I must love you.

I'm coming home on labor day.   Could I trouble you for the
following evening, space, the following evening, the following
evening, space, space, the following evening, space, the
following evening, space, the following evening, after which
I sha'n't disturb you until fall houseparty sometime in October.
I love you.

why do I love you?

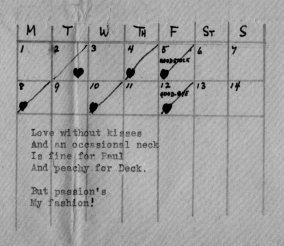

Love without kisses
And an occasional neck
Is fine for Paul
And peachy for Deck.

But passion's
My fashion!

Have a cigarette.   Smoke it while playing Why Do I Love You.
Think of ME dammit!

October 15, 1942

Dear Woofy,

I'm truly sorry you can't come--it means, of course, that this party will be about fifty per-cent less fun than I had expected. As things have now developed in the face of the emergency, I have a blind date coming from Vassar, the sister of Brother Tod Knowles '45, Juliet. If she doesn't turn out well, I shall endeavor to exhaust her quickly. This, if successfully carried out, will make me a legitimate (by agreement made in the last house meeting) wolf. If she is wonderful, the first move will be to get her brother out of the way--a touchy situation.

Conclusion reached two days ago follows: If the Army is as short of men as they say, I have no business attempting to wiggle out of the draft when it hits me--November 11th, or sooner if the 18-20 bill goes through. It may well be passed by the time you read this. On the strength of my being a chemist (or thereabouts), I plan to ask for a deferment until February. Then, during Christmas vacation, I'll enlist in whatever branch of the service I choose. Cornell will give me credit for the term, which means that I'll have Senior standing when I return after the Peace is won.

At this point, I can't give a damn for anything. I've got weltschmerz like never before. We pledged 15 very nifty freshmen, including a likable Kieth Nesbitt from the Hoosier state. Mother and Dad sent some Sassafrass tea from a weekend in Brown County. I had it served at the Junior table--it was terrible; I had to drink everybody's. Can't find a football schedule. Penn is about Thanksgiving time. Cornell has no team at all. The point is that I've got to see you.

                                Love,
                                Kurt-

November 1, 1942

Dearest Woofy:

This is to clear up a couple of points, and to reestablish communications with you. I find your letters quite often a pleasant tonic. If you don't write soon, I'll have poured a fortune into long distance telephone calls.

I was given a physical examination for the ERC this morning, in which the health of every damned part of me was startlingly verified. I passed and will be sworn in Thursday afternoon--beating Draft Board #14 to the punch by six days. The plan is this: regardless of my draft status, I shall leave school at the close of this semester to enlist in the branch of the Army which appeals the most.

As for Pennsylvania...well, I can't make it. They've given us a scant Thanksgiving Vacation of Thursday, November 26th (day of the game). This means that we wont see each other until Christmas--a grim situation, mighty tough on morale. Put me on record as wanting New Years Eve with you.

For all I know, some completely wonderful guy has been rushing the pants off of you with moderate success. If so, I should like to hear a few details.

The Sun continues to function...I was elected to Aleph Samach, Junior honorary society...Mary Glossbrenner has had a serious nervous breakdown...Cupitt is in the air corps... Bill Hughes is going to be drafted...the Navy has taken over the men's dorms...we pledged 16 freshmen...I hit the Dean of Men with a bicycle while riding it in the Alpha Delt living room...my blind date from Vassar had a lip like a button-hole and a personality and IQ of a young eel.

Kurt-Jr

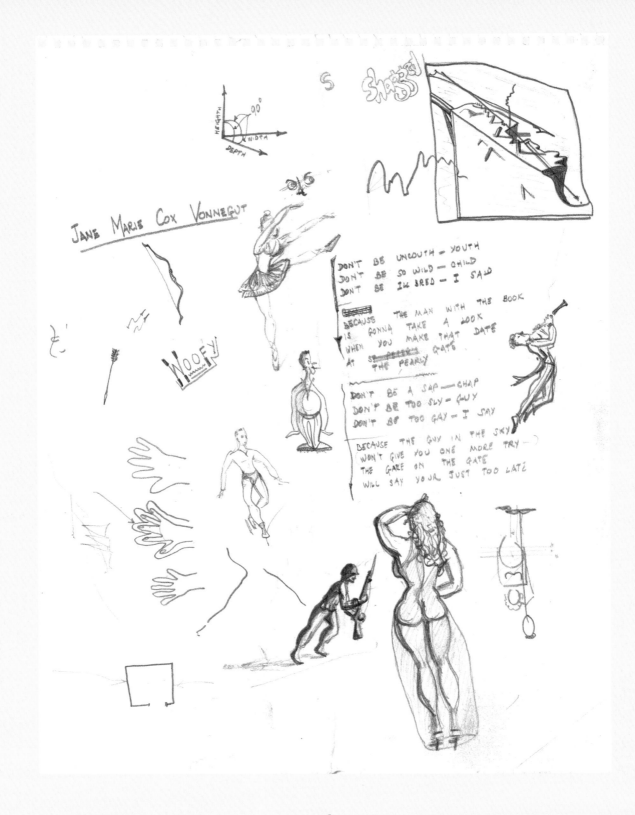

JANE MARIE COX VONNEGUT

WOOFY

DON'T BE UNCOUTH — YOUTH
DON'T BE SO WILD — CHILD
DON'T BE ILL BRED — I SAID

BECAUSE THE MAN WITH THE BOOK
IS GONNA TAKE A LOOK
WHEN YOU MAKE THAT DATE
AT ST. PETERS GATE
THE PEARLY

DON'T BE A SAP — CHAP
DON'T BE TOO SLY — GUY
DON'T BE TOO GAY — I SAY

BECAUSE THE GUY IN THE SKY
WON'T GIVE YOU ONE MORE TRY —
THE GATE ON THE GATE
WILL SAY YOUR JUST TOO LATE

November 15, '42

Dear Woofy:

It wasn't too pleasant hearing Bill Hughes
make big plans for the Penn week-end.   Cornell
stands a wonderful chance of beating her traditional rival--I stand small chance of seeing you
again for at least many months. Though it's still
a matter of faculty debate, I doubt that I'll be
home for Christmas vacation. At the end of this
term, January fifteenth, I'll go home to enlist
as a regular. I'm already a private in the Army--
number 12835987, apparently not the first to join.

The vitality has left Cornell, and I've set
a new high for low in my studies. I should never
have set out to become a highly specialized (degree of which is directly proportional to the shall-
owness of life) technician. I'm glad I've dabbled
in the sciences, for I can understand and interpret
a great and interesting number of things which would
otherwise be forever mysterious. Such a scientific
sympathy is, I think, certainly in keeping with the
times. Through it my chances as a journalist are
enhanced. I welcome the change which will soon
startle me, for it will mark a new phase--I shall
have passed the larval stage. That outside world
is going to be a helluva lot of fun if I live long
enough to play around in it.

There goes that big yet little, hot yet cold
feeling in my lungs again--I described it for you
once...

Love,

Kurt-Jr.

37

Dear Woofy:

Naturally your recent letter ripped my heart
from my wounded breast (poetic license). My Princeton friend, Morgan Bird (It's a Small World Department:
he kissed you good-bye just before the Triangle Club
pulled out of Union Station some two New Year's Eves
ago), and the rest of our picked squad of All-American
Barflies spent the week-end in a Raleigh hotel suite.
This contest of giants ended in a draw though I was
awarded a decoration for valor beyond the call of
duty for making a breakfast of beer Monday morning.

So many of my friends are commissioned that I
can't help feeling a little distinctive with absolutely nothing on my uniform but buttons. Ryan and
I are very happy as privates. How long this atti-
tude will hold out is a sober question. Methinks it
had better be durable enough to last for duration and
six months. In a couple of weeks I'll know if I'm
to be an officer, a college student, or a dead duck.

Lovey, I know what hell you've been going through
being absolutely true to me. I want you to know that
I appreciate it. Abstainance makes the heart grow
fonder. These xxxx once cool, tapering and artistic
hands have been initiated into the more brutal myster-
ies of Ju-Jitsu. I am now a match for any woman

twice my size.   I shall probably be back late in July.
I shall probably try to see you as much as possible--
or as much of you as possible.   Are you glad?
If you want to break up an otherwise morbid summer
I don't care if you want to get married.   I, Kurt
Vonnegut Jr.,am financially independent and in a
position to afford a one-week honeymoon in the Semin-
ole Hotel.

    Apropos, are you ever going to get married?
I am willing to fill out any required forms in dup-
licate, triplicate and quintuplicate for your hand
and all accessories thereof; not now, but sometime.
You don't object to my playing with the idea, do you?

    Write me a letter, sweet mamma.

Kurt

To Woofy

Perhaps a fraction

Of sheer abstraction

expressed in action

in loves own faction ...

or fate's disaster

in mucoid plaster ;

or fate's own master ,

expressed in blood and alabaster ;

~~Thexsextakiexpxiatinate~~

Vexed by the sex hex,

The baren decks of ships that sex wreck~~s~~

Roll and take a droll toll

Of myriad foal souls

Yes...of myriad gentle foal ~~xsaks~~ souls

Gentle foul and foal ~~xks~~ souls

That sprawl on the beach ...

This beach on which we stand--

Sprawl to bbeach

To bleach for ~~xs~~ our lifetime?

Nay, silly child, for our lifetime is

eternity...

bones ade far too perishable to persist so long as eternity.

,,,,,,,.synonymous

1943:
WAR AT HOME

IN JANUARY 1943, KURT DECIDED NOT TO GO BACK TO COR-
nell. Though he was deeply anti-war, he felt that World War II was one
that had to be fought. He enlisted in the army rather than wait to be
drafted, or expelled from Cornell. He was rejected once for his pneumonia but tried again, successfully this time, in March.

Kurt trained at the University of Tennessee in Knoxville and Fort
Hayes in Columbus, Ohio. In June, he qualified for a program called the
Army Specialized Training Program (ASTP), which enabled him to
study introductory mechanical engineering at the Carnegie Institute of
Technology in Pittsburgh. In qualifying for this program, Kurt was
under the impression that he would not be sent overseas to fight the war
on the front lines, which was a great relief to his family.

SEPTEMBER FOUND HIM continuing furlough coursework at the
University of Tennessee.

Jane was beginning her senior year. In addition to Kurt, she had several suitors with names like Bates and Kendall, but her academic life was

more important to her than dating and letter writing. Kurt's letters were outnumbering hers six to one. He would date other women from time to time, but that seemed more like a ploy to get Jane's attention than anything else. He had time on his hands. She did not. In addition to the pressure of her studies, Jane was stressed about her mother, who had just suffered another mental collapse, which Jane did not think Riah would survive.

OH HAPPY HAPPY ST. VALENTINE'S DAY
♡ ♡ ♡

IN THE FACE OF COMPETITION
I'M AFRAID MY LOT'S PERDITION
FOR I'M MOVING TO THE U. OF TENNESSEE.
IT'S OFF THE BUSY HIGHWAY
SO YOUR CHANCE OF GOING MY WAY
SEEMS PRETTY DAMN REMOTE TO EVEN ME.

BUT BE MY VALENTINE ANYWAY,
JUST FOR THE PLAIN HELL OF IT.

THOUGH THE TRAINING IS TERRIFIC,
I WOULD RATHER BE PROLIFIC.
ARMY LIFE IS DAMN NEAR SEXLESS;
DAMMIT, I WANT SEX FOR BREAKFAST.
—♡—
WHILE THEY'RE TEACHING ME DESTRUCTION,
I FIND MY MIND ON REPRODUCTION.
ARMY LIFE IS DAMN NEAR SEXLESS;
DAMMIT I WANT SEX FOR BREAKFAST.

KURT

LOVE LOVE LOVE LOVE LOVE LOVE LOVE LOVE LOVE LOVE LOVE LOVE LOVE LOVE LOVE LOVE LOVE LOVE LOVE LOVE LOVE LOVE LOVE LOVE LOVE LOVE LOVE LOVE LOVE LOVE LOVE LOVE LOVE LOVE LOVE LOVE LOVE LOVE LOVE LOVE LOVE LOVE LOVE LOVE LOVE LOVE LOVE

Dear Woofy:

    Perchance you've received my Valentine
and are dying to know where I may be reached
that you may dispatch a flood of gratitude
embellished with those little tendernesses
that lovers whisper on spring nights. O.K.,
lovey, I'm at the University of Tennessee,
Knoxville.   If Tennessee were to try
to secede from the Union again I don't
think anyone would try to stop them.
The Holy Trinity of Methodist, Baptist and
Bootlegger are keeping Knoxville dry. Old
  Breath Jersey Bonded Fusil Oil may be
bought from Bellhop #2 at the Farragut
Hotel for $7.00 a pint.   I had a bellyful
of denatured and therefore legal beer last
night. My only sensation of debauch was
that my belly was full and that I
belched voluminously and that those belches
billowed and chewed at the mucous membranes
of my sinus with yeasty carbon-dioxide
teeth.

    So far, the Methodists, Baptists and
Whoremongers have not made womankind a
premium item. However, the ricky-tick-lick device
which I blindly believed to be a mild and

reasonably satisfactory jitterbug is strictly laughable here. Terpsichore picked up a case of D.T.'s on corn whiskey and moved from the mountains into Knoxville. Barbara spent a patient Wednesday and Thursday night teaching me the basic hot licks. As you may suspect, it ended in harsh words and gnashing of teeth. She married a sailor yesterday and I went to Bellhop #2 on my knees; not because of Barbara but because I got tired of looking at things just as they are. I quote:

> Here's to a bottle of Whiskey,
> So sparkling and so clear;
> It ain't as sweet as a pretty girl's lips,
> But a damned site more sincere

My brother got caught, and quite nicely too, in the national plague of hot-pants. Bow and Bernie were home when I was. Good Lord but she's lovely.

If all goes according to plan I'll be busted out of here shortly. Show interest and I'll keep you posted. Any chance of your being home the first week in May?

I LOVE YOU

Kurt

March 3, 1943

Dear Woofy-:

    I'm due back at Fort Hayes in about ten days, at
which time--I can't help feeling--you, as well as the
Army, will form an oppinion of me. Prepared for the
worst, it may be that I shall have to hide my face when,
in ten years or so, little Terpsichore asks, "Daddy, what
did you do in the last war?" An alternative might be to
raise my family outside of Indianapolis, and lie like hell.
However, I may be accepted this time. At first, I thought
they'd discovered I was a sex maniac, but decided you would-
n't have been so mean as to broadcast our sordid little
secret. It turns out that once when I was an itty-bitty
feller, and thought the only difference between men and
women was that men smelled of tobacco--especially grand-
father--, I contracted a slight case of TB, which healed
immediately but left a few scars. When I got my Army physical, the spots showed up along with traces of pneumonia.
((Am I boring you?)) They doped it out that I had a raging
case of TB. Dr. Steele says they're crazy, so instead of
getting kicked clear out I'm to report back for a recheck.
Hitz got rejected because his spots (everybody's got 'em)
were too big. Mayhap this will disqualify me. All the
Doctors around here think it's a damned silly ruling as
the spots--so long as they're healed--represent no sort of
menace, or flaw in a person's physical condition. The rule
is about to be dissolved, I hear. Through the cooperation
of Mr. Kellum, City Editor of the Star, I have offers of
three reporting jobs on small papers--the place to start--
if I get a final veto. In any event, ten days or so should
see me leaving home never to return a dependent...it says
here.

    There's no one left in town with whom I can cry into
beer. Thus, I've resolved into a closet drinker and weep-
er. Both elements are flowing in quantity at this moment.
Tommy Dorsey isn't helping any with his memory tunes. At
this point, "Sweety" becomes indispensible...

    Sweety, you're by far the best of all my memory tunes.
Despite what either of us says to the contrary--and we seem
to damned frequently--we've had some pretty wonderful times.
((This is tripe. I've got something to say, but damned if I
know what it is.)) This is about the idea: let's love each
other. Until you reply, I refuse to start. I want you for
my mate. ((The temperature hits 45° and I'm in a mating mood.))
There are plenty of other fish in the ocean but I'll be damned
((redundant, ain't it?)) if I'll sleep with a flounder. ((You'll
be damned if I'll sleep with you--eh?)) I like you very, very
much. I'm fond of you. You are nice. What's more, I'm
nice. Please confirm this last oppinion.

    Love,

    KURT

Thank you, Woofy, for a wonderful, wonderful long letter. This is a poor and foolish reply.

Dear Woofy:

Our letters have become stereotyped in that for the past two years they have begun with Dear and ended with love—no more, no less. Taken literally they carry the most affectionate and warm sentiment that can pass between two people. Dear Woofy—reflect a moment on that. How wonderfully fortunate you are to be held dear; not liked, admired or adored but held to be a life-giving element in another person's life— you are dear to me. What a triumph of truth in a world of secrets the word dear is. To found a science, with the word dear as a basis; startling fields have been discovered and put to practical uses with foundations almost as obscure. Dear—yes, yes; there's a hint of something big and bright and flood-like. What? I am only the father of the study—primative, naiive. I know the sun is warm and beautiful and that it appears and disappears in the distance. That much I am permitted to know about the sun. I love it, fear it and think about it but learn no more. You are dear to me.

And love: well, that is more animal, and as one chipmunk loves another chipmunk I love you. Life must get better if it is to go on. Were we to marry life would go on and our children would make it better. That is good and in the hilarious sport of making wild love in the process of manufacturing super-babies I can think of no more agreeable team-mate. Orm Hessler used to say that when he and Connie Bond were married they would play football every night and Connie would lose every game. Yes, I love you.

Please, Woofy, don't mean "My God how he leans on me," because that isn't exactly so. If you love Suicide Sam as much as you say, don't worry about how I'll feel or about how the course of my life is likely to run as a result of it. Bernard is 29 and Bow is 22. Chances are my bride is a rove of it. This, along with the conviction that oblivion is the ultimate, tempers my emotions very nicely. I will be in Philadelphia April 29th, en route to Boston. I've damn near got to see you then, Woofy, so please be there if you can.

I've a young married cousin in Knoxville, Susan Mengel:—

① Mueller ② Vonnegut ③ Mengel ④ Rauch ⑤ Glossbrenner ⑥ Fauvre ⑦ Lindener
⑧ Schnull — not one of 'em left.

She has made life in this God-forsaken spot a great deal more bearable. This isn't much of a letter, I admit. Maybe I'll write another soon.

You have outgrown Wally, I think. Tell me more about Salty Sid that I may be relieved of the suspicion that there might have been some prophesy in my booze-born oratory of two-hundred sunday mornings ago. Methinks you would make a career of being a student as a line of, in your case, least resistance. That crack about Salty Sid was a low blow. Please forgive it — I don't mean it.

There is damn little that can be done for humanity. You can give them potato peelers, sulpha drugs and bridges but spiritually and morally they are very low on the scale of evolution and evolutional advances take millions of years. We must be patient. Love. Kurt

Dear Woofy--darling, dammit:

I saw the Northern lights for the first
time in my life tonight. It was pretty much
like kissing you, and just as rare.

"To be perfectly honest with you, I don't
expect my love for you to last any great length
of time." ...Bravely said by Kurt Vonnegut
during the assault on Jane Cox of August 15th,
1940. Spoken with conceit, back-from-college
stuff; trying to be honest with you, I lied
like hell to myself. The halves of my split
personality got together over beer this evening. We have the answer now. We love you,
really love you, wont be happy until you love
us, and will feel that way for several years
to come.

I keep wanting to shoot people: Paul,
Deck, you, me, in that order. It's my turn.
Maybe I'll kill a bottle instead.

Excessive suppression
Brings pangs of depression.

Passion's
The fashion!

The animal in me deserves to
be in the dog-house for what
he's been thinking about all
day.

U.S. ARMY

June 23rd...'43

Dearest Woof:

Thank you, Sweety, for writing. I thought
that you were probably having a pretty rough
time of it.   I'm mightily sorry, Woof, and
wish to heaven I could be there to take your
mind off matters--if such be my powers.

Methinks I'll be home for one hectic week
soon after July 15th...at which time I'll pay
you court.   In training with me is a color-
ful character, one MacCarthy, who was discharged from the Marines for having gone over
the hill four times.   His testimony is that
our basic training is easily as rough as that
which he underwent as a leatherneck. Perhaps
our most spectacular adventure to date is that
of crawling on our bellies for 150 yards under machine-gun fire, skimming a sickening
two feet above the ground.   "Keep your goddam
ass down, Vonnegut!" --and down it damned well
stayed. Movie cameras hummed busily as my
life hung by a thread, for "See Here, Private
Hargrove" is being filmed in this, the setting
for Marion's epic.   In order that theatre-
goers not be bored by the sequence in which
my posterior figures, dynamite was sprinkled
generously over me.   Only my laundryman knows
how frightened I really was.

In a few days I'll be leaving for the
grand finale, ten days in the field under combat privations--: i.e., home is where you dig
it and dinner is what you can dig out of a can
with a bayonette.

Though I've fought the transition with
determination and cunning, I'm in wonderful
physical condition. Still to be confirmed

is the conviction that I've become a tough
sonofabitch.

Anti-climax is that I'm to return to
college for 44 weeks of specialized training.
Where and what I'm to study will be decided
after basic.   Pardon this boyish impulse, but
I shall campaign for a college near to wherever
you may be.   If possible, please advise me on
this point.   One happy day I shall be a Sergeant Technician; fairly fancy in lieu of a
gold bar, and, incidentall_y, an entre thereto.

Kurt Vonnegut, Jr.,in uniform, as you
might guess, is not a sight to stimulate War
Bond sales. My plan is to retreat into flannels once in Broad Ripple and points north.
Another selfish plot is to take you and a case
of beer on our third annual cruise to the
Wharf House. Such an exploit seems a lovely
dream; subject matter for seventy fitful nights.

As to your writing some work of note: my
conviction has ever been that the depth, breadth
and color of your emotions and imagination
are the elements of a powerful novel. For
these things I hold you an awesome thing and
love you dearly.

++++++++++++++++

Youth is such a wonderful thing, it
seems a shame to waste it on the young--GBS

Love,

Kurt-

THIS SIDE OF CARD IS FOR ADDRESS

Woofy Cox
Swarthmore College
Swarthmore, Pennsylvania

-o-o-o-

54

VONNEGUT CHARM SCHOOLS, INC.
Indianapolis - Ithaca - Fort Sill - Tokyo - Valhalla

Dear Miss Cox:

I've read your reply (undated) several times, and I must
confess that for the first time in a decade of straightening
tangled lives and reviving crushed blossoms I feel inadequate.
Yours is indeed a problem: one I should hesitate to approach,
so deeply is it rooted, were I not convinced that my job here
on this strife-torn world is to spread what little sun-shine
I can.

From the typography of your note I glean that you are a
moderately artistic woman with a desire to be different, but
a terribly nervous creature, wound up tighter than an idiot's
watch. I find your letter facetious though you are in desperate need of help. You make my task the more difficult by put-
ing up smoke screens, as it were. You cannot hide that bitter
ache in your heart, my dear, until we erase it forever!

There is no such word as can't. You can and will win
me back if you persevere. There is no place in this world for
defeatism. Men, and in some isolated cases even women, are gov-
erned by pride. Indeed, without it, nobody would ever get angry
at anybody which seems to be the whole point of living. Your
attempt to win me back was damned feeble, if you'll pardon my
skipping over professional barriers. It is an unforgivable breach
of taste to figuretively kick a dear acquaintance in the trous-
ers. If need be, I shall be more explicit in my next message, for
which I hope you write.

I am on 24 hours' call, which has yet to come. I've practically lost my mind doing nothing. There are no girls left in
this town who have an I.Q. over 120 coupled with intellectual
curiosity as to what the inside of a bar looks like and what pleasure
people get from drinking.

Love... KURT.

55

Dear Woof:

I had another fine date with Nance last night. One more, and I'd be head-over-heels in love with her, so last night was the last of a pleasant, mildly tight series. You have a standing invitation to stay with her, here in Pittsburgh, and long before my assignment is completed at Tech I hope you take her up on it at least once. One time, when you were very low, Woof, I remember your worrying about your feminine friends: that is, your lack of really good and loyal ones. I'm pretty sure that worry was baseless, but I'd like to point out that Nance likes you one helluva lot, and is, whether you've ever looked at it that way or not, one of your best friends. You two are the most wonderful pair of girls I've come across. And I've been from Memphis to Mobile; from Natchez to St. Joe...

Here's that idea again, and if ever I'm commissioned I promise I'll propose (Lt. and Mrs. J. C. Adams have now been in dreamland for eight months)——I'd love to be that happy!). Nance and I have, without consulting you or Buck (something like the Atlantic Charter without Stalin or Chiang), planned Heaven ("Everybody talkin' 'bout Heaven ain't goin' there") for the four of us. Would you like to live in Charleston, one block from Calhoun's grave and within sight of Ft. <u>Sumpter</u>? That's just about where we figured Heaven was. To be exact, it's in a cottage (with a studio) in a hidden patio in the finest, and oldest part of town. Not a church in the neighborhood is under 200 years old. I just happened upon it! The entrance is an inconspicuous little arch, guarded by an antique wrought-iron gate, between a fine wine shop and a musty book store. Both are tiny and neither bothers to advertize beyond a small, neat shingle. Both sell the fine, the very old, and the deliciously delicate. Their clientel is a fraternity to which only the connaisseour may belong.

→ G. Washington slept next door

← To the Bay

Within the gate is a long path between the buildings, and from this path you can peek between shutters into the ~~musty~~ back room of the wine shop where those rare bottles, which weren't smashed by the roar of the Union naval guns firing on blockade runners, still collect dust. (Speaking of blockade runners — and hence Rhett Butler —: Scarlet O'hara went to finishing school in Fayetteville, one mile from Fort Bragg.)) The path opens into a patio, in which stands a giant old oak and a lush green-grass carpet. A not-so-historical cottage (it's always summer in sleepy Charleston) snoozes in the shade of the oak: room for four merry young people with tremendous appitites for happiness.

This may bore you. It's been so long since we've been together that I've grown self-conscious about what I say. I must miss you, Woof, because I'm miserably lonely with hundreds of good friends about me. During one of our rowdy "in-love-with-each-other" phases it was your habit to pique me by asking, "why do you

love me?" I've finally hit
on a rational answer and
I think it's the right one.
I have a number of wild
dreams which come and go
with the green in the
leaves. Once conceived I tell
you about them. If they're
good dreams you take them
up with a flood of enthusiasm and we're very soon
shrieking to each other about
them in a transport of
delight much greater than if
the dream were realized.
Then we sink back, logically,
in each others' arms, happily
exhausted by a swift trip
to heaven and back.

I asked Nance how many
times she had seen me
make you cry. I hated to
hear her say four. This,
I hope is a step toward
maturity, Woof—; I pray to
God I never make you cry
again.

I never enjoyed writing
a letter so much as this
one. It flowed from me
without a murmur.

Love,
Kurt.

My Dear Miss Cox:

    Your failure to respond has led me to con-
sider dropping you from the course.   Please understand that my helping you in your hour of
need is impossible without your coöperation.
    However, at no extra charge and as a
possible incentive I submit a question for the
day: If you marry Bates, what will you do with
me?

                        Respectfully,
                        Kurt Vonnegut, Jr,
                        First Violinist, Emeritus

Dearest Woofy:

I hate to see you, my someday girl of many a dream, slip away into the shadows. Whether tomorrow is that someday or if it is many years from now I don't know, but it, and those that follow will be better than any I've known. At the precise moment that God settles back into his easy chair in Heaven and lights up a good cigar, you and I will fall wonderfully deep in love and tread happily on pink clouds forever after:— that is that one, that some-day.

Visualization of you and me becomes more blurred and fairyland-like as time's fog closes behind me. We've been gloriously happy, haven't we? And weren't we in love? Were we meant for each other for just an instant? I imply no answer to any of these questions—they are musings. My mental state in thinking about us must be something like that of a person who has lost his memory:—a glimmer of the past, a flood of warm pleasure; the glimmer fades and with it dies the pleasure, leaving only a faint and melancholy longing.

Sometime-girl, have you gone? —

Kurt

October 17, 1943

Dearest Woof:

My roommate, Don Cooper, was having dates with a girl twenty-one when he was seventeen. One night he tried to take her blouse off. "You wouldn't know what to do if I let you," she said. Coop admits she was right, and, allegorically speaking, I feel as foolish as he must have. I want something. It looks wonderful from the outside. I've raised holy hell to get it, yet I'm extremely uncertain as to what it is or what it's for. (At this point our little allegory gets ludicrous, but mayhap you see the point.)

You made a clearer point in explaining about your letters. I'm sorry, Sweety. "I'm tired of that feeling so I may as well forget it and be myself" poked through whatever barrier there was and let flow the loveliest letter I've ever read. You wonder why I still love you so. It's something like the "Big Inch" oil pipeline running from West to East: there's a powerful pump every few miles to keep the pressure up and the oil flowing. If ever my love has been at a low ebb, something like this letter in front of me, or our

walk into Broad Ripple comes
along—to keep the pressure
up and the oil flowing.
  Now that I have your
blouse off—i.e, you're coming
to Pittsburgh, I'm not sure
what to do. As has been
our custom—word by word,
step by step we'll augment
our fund of fragmentary
happiness; until one day we'll
die, with an epitaph like
this, for those persons whose
curiosity leads them into
obscure parts of a cemetary
to read:

  Here lie two people
to whom many good and
bad things came. They
built a lovely and worthwhile
life from splinters of pleasure.
They were wonderfully happy.
They were sorry they had
to go.

  I'll meet you at the
station.

              Love,
              Kurt

Dear Woofy:

I spent what was left of the night and most of the day in 696. Without my having said so, the William Penn assumed that you were my wife and so had provided — I suppose you noticed — a double bed. If I hadn't been so damned dead dog tired I wouldn't have slept in the big empty thing. We had left the window open wide so 696 was doubly cold. What an empty, sickening feeling, sweety. Most people who love music started in that vein because of a big gloomy hole in their lives. I don't hear music, and I mean all kinds of music, very often. But occasionally a few sweet strains seep in — from a passing car radio, a victrola in a nearby apartment, a piano in a second story music school. It fills the gap for a glowing time chip. That's what our — what, eight hours? — together was in my life. A medley of Liebestraum, Basin Street Blues, Auld langsyne, Sweet Adeline, Finlandia, Tuxedo Junction, Melody in F, Schubert's Serenade, My Blue Heaven, and The Nutcracker Suite.
Remember when you

made me turn my back to you
— before you gave me the picture.
You asked me what I was
thinking. "Darling, darling, darling,
darling" ran through my mind
until it sounded like bells. Those
bells kept ringing until they
joined spirits with the big bell
on the 3:47 and clanged out
of the station, into the night.

J'espere vous pris le Prix
de Paris. My one mortal fear
is that, once rolling, you'll be
fiendishly successful and that
starting out wedded bliss in
a little shack will be an unthink-
able setback.

The pressure is up and the
oil flowing at a great rate in
The Big Inch.

I love you, Woofy. There's
many a sonofabitch who's said
as much and meant it in his
own Juke Box way, but I'm the
only one who loves you for what
you ought to be loved, the only
one whose bulk of ambition, direction
and pleasure would be embodied
in you.

Kurt

HAPPY BIRTHDAY

Happy Birthday

What if a much of a dream of
    a girl
Brings love to a too lonely guy;
Leaves him believing that she's
the one to give truth to the
        human lie;
Brings music to clatter and
    dream to wake;
Brings substance to shadow,
    mend to break?
Whose love is a mountain,
    devotion a sea:
It's they who cry there
    is only one.

What if the neat of a sweet
    girl sighs,
Her heart she will never know;
Holds her passion a dangerous
      thing;
Stifles past in a dead ago;
Brings can't to should be
    and never to must;
Brings was to always and
    almost to just.
Only space and time and
      matter—;
The more love dies the
    less we live.

Dear Woof;

I'm coming home October 30th. Methinks you'll be leaving about the same time. From your letters I perceive you've changed a great deal. I'd like to see just what you are like. I used to know.

You no doubt know how abstract my "I love you" is — and it doesn't make too damned much difference, because it's been beating on deaf ears for a couple of years now. One peculiar feature of our relation-ship (whatever in hell that is) is that you are the one person in this world to whom I like to write. If ever I do write anything of length — good or bad — it will be written with you in mind. I honestly don't know why. I doubt if it's love. As nearly as I can figure you're the best friend I've got.

Dear Woof:
    Your wild and enthusiastic orgies
of dead silence drive me a
little nuts. Writing you has become as futile and frustrating
as sprinkling handbills saying
"Jesus is Coming."
    Lamblike as you know and
love me to be, the one atom
of ill-humored Tiger in me
roars this bitch—: Goddammit;
you're the punkest correspond-
ent I've got. Whyfore, articulate
one? Many's the time I've heard
you say you liked and wanted
to write. Seldom's the time
I've doubted it but often's
the time I've wondered when.
    We've had and will have mighty
little time together for a stinking
long time. Maybe you can understand
my urgency,—rather, call it curiosity.
You have the habit of keeping me
in the dark about everything
connected with yourself, and upon
our rare meetings have a huge
number of developements to relate.
—For all I know that pile
of dead·letters from my note
book bore obscenities on their
backs. I forgot to look. You can
see why I never mailed them.
   Love,
       Kurt

About November 8th
1943
for sure.

Dear Woof:

    I guess I see what you mean, our relationship being the most intricate, complex problem you've run across. But I'm damned if I know what makes you think it so or how it came to be a rat's nest. It would be a help to me if you would try to explain. As I get the implication—: In view of a rather lengthy and offimes spectacular courting on my part you should, by every law of man, God and nature love me. But conscientiously strain as you will in that direction, results are not forthcoming.

    To date, my frequent pleas to adore and cherish me and only me, if answered in the affirmative would and could wreak not the slightest change in our ways of life. This is a perfect cue for a crack which I'm surprised you never experimentally made: "Kurt, I love you with all my heart — So what the hell?" Had you said that I would been amazed into a stupid and bamboozled silence. Wooing has an undeniable basic goal (we never denied it) — anywhere from fifteen minutes to a lifetime of nights in bed together. I've had you in mind for the lifetime assignment for quite a while — and for the fifteen minutes if you can spare the time. Every time I've brought this matter to your attention I've had fifteen cents in my pocket, two dollar's worth of beer in my stomach and the prospects of a beach-comber. I think that if ever I get to a point where marriage looks like a sound thing you would marry me. That's pretty smug — but what the hell, I could make you happier than anyone else you've ever met. You'd be a damn fool to turn me down. In reply: you are to do nothing, to say nothing, to act in no particular way — until the white light of wisdom shines on your heart. I may have to concede that that will be never.

    I'll make the requested effort to love someone more than you. In skeleton form I'll send you a chapter in what may be an amusing tale after each week-end. If you're enthusiastic about my falling passionately in love mayhap your adroit coaching can help. Next July I may be assigned to Europe as a commissioned engineer. Providing I haven't found some wonderful girl, twice as good as you'll ever hope to be, lovely, volcanically sexy, fond of beer, music and me, I'll ask you to come with me. However, with forty week-ends and the delectable young plums of Pittsburgh before me I wouldn't count on it.

Huzzah and tally-ho, lovey. With lewd wit and lecherous glances I'm off to torment voluptuous women and to drive timid virgins wild.

Love,

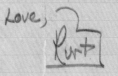

I liked your letter. Write again soon. You probably don't like this one. I do. I think it's the nuts.

Dear Woof:

I seem to put you in such a state of
torment and your pleas to be let alone are
so sincere and inoffensive that I shall stop
heckling you with love letters and such stuff.
Providing one thing: that you explain for my serenity,
also to be considered, just why you feel that ours
is one of the most intricate and complex relation-
ships you've come across in your short span.
This is a tough assignment, I know, as your
letters indicate turmoil and indecision over the
peculiar broth I've brewed. But please try
to be as concise as you can. Methinks your
implication has been that you should love
me but can't — and if you did, what
could it possibly mean to either of us at
a time like this? That's an intelligent way
to look at it — if you do look at it that way
— and I don't mind particularly. You say that
one day a great white light may shine on your
heart. I guess that means that when this
damn war is over and I have something with
which to build a small house and a promise
in the future of wings to be added to it
— that will be the time to start my
sales talk.

In the hope that I may accumulate something
fairly amusing and lengthy I plan to log
my weekly attempts to fall in love and
send them to you. You are to save them
for me. That way, you can watch my
progress, coach me and be of immense help.

Your letter is dog-eared before me. It's a
good one, Woof. I'd say you were considerably
more alive than in haunted Indianapolis.

That modern lit course sounds like a
helluva lot of fun. I'm familiar — I think —
with a couple of those you mentioned: Chekhov,
Cowboy (am I wrong?) Will James, Ibsen (see G. B. Shaw)

whom I don't like so well (at least in the translation I got), and Sam Butler. Chekhov is sort of a surrealistic realist. I've a fat volume of his short stories which I read from cover to cover last year. Two I've never forgot: "Sleepy" (I believe) and one involving a doctor who is called from his young son's deathbed by a man who insists his wife is dying. The doctor leaves his dead son and prostrate wife to go with the excited young man. The young man's wife had feigned sickness to get him out of the house and had run off with her lover while he was gone. "The Way of All Flesh" is all I've read by Butler. What else has he written?

Love,

Kurt

Woof— Goddam but I'd love to see you again. Could you stop by Pittsburgh on your way home, Christmas? I may make it to Philly some week-end soon. I'd like a date with you Christmas night providing you're not so goddam much in love with Toothbrush Terry that you can't see straight,

                              six minutes later

Dear Woof:

        This may be pretty close to what I tried to say in
the other letter.   This is the impression I get from Cox
kisses.

                Your friendship much can make me blest,
                O why that bliss destroy!
                Why urge the only, one request
                You know I will deny!

                Your thought, if Love must harbour there,
                Conceal it in that thought;
                Nor cause me from my bosom tear
                The very friend I sought.

                                --Robert Burns

        What can I do to be lovable?   You're hell to get along
with!   Damn, damn, damn.

Dear Woofy,

My conscientious effort to fall in love with someone else has left me broke, flunking, and now with a severe head cold. Seated in the shambles of what once was a healthy, happy and solvent young life, I survey that which has recently past. Phoebe, Eleanor, Diana, Nancy—: I did those things to and with them I've done to you, and there's no denying it's been a big time;* but grunt and strain as I will I cant love them. They're all strictly good—i.e. you would approve. Nancy is the most promising. I plan to keep trying to love her. One trouble with the campaign is that it's cold here. My love for you was tempered in the white-heat of July and August and seasoned in the embers of Indian summer.

This paragraph—were I to write it—would be a glib and syrupy stew of alliteration, allegory, simile, parody, counterpoint and hemstitching telling of a new and novel way I've found to love you. Such a distracting piece of blurb will be sent to you very soon if you don't answer my question of a few weeks ago—Please, Woof, what's the score?

Love

Kurt—

Dearest Woofy:

I'll come out a heavy loser—(that is, I'll probably never ever hear from your sweet self again)—if I don't reinitiate our so called corespondence: "co", meaning "joint;" "respondence" meaning the act of responding; to a given stimulus—in this case a written message of some sort.

A type stimulus of that sort might be: Jane, darling, know full well that I miss you. These are warm days and convivial nights but I am spoiled for having lived in four dimensions; for having seen the invisible rhapsodic colors at either end of the spectrum; for having heard the thunder and the shriek of the octaves below and above the range of the human ear.

Then again that might strike you as being like drowning in fruit salad so I try mystery: Sim and her obedient satalites move in their orderly elliptical orbits. Her boiling valleys, molten rivers and furious volcanoes congeal beneath a tranquil blanket of soft white ashes. Parasite Earth grows cold. A billion human bodies lie frozen rock-hard under a windless blue-green prairie of ice. Wise little men, basking in the hot verility of a younger star, look and know that there cannot be life on Earth.

Chances are that you might be most likely to write if I were to adopt a light vein: The "She's Went and Gone to the Pentagon, Left Me Flat to be a Bureaucrat Blues" have bogged down pending more particulars from you. Also, there will be considerable relief felt in these quarters when Mother Nature pronounces our horrendous assault on joint immortality through progeny a mechanical fiasco.

Love,
Pfc. Kurt Vonnegut, Jr.
xxxxxxxxxxxx

—

1944:
SHIPPING OUT

BY MID-APRIL 1944, THE ASTP PROGRAM WAS CANCELED, as troops were needed for D-Day. Kurt was assigned to the 106th "Golden Lion" Infantry Division, 423rd Regiment, and ordered to Camp Atterbury in Indiana to train as an intelligence and reconnaissance scout, which involved interpreting maps and setting up advance observation posts.

On May 14, while Kurt was home on leave from Camp Atterbury, his mother, Edith, died of a barbiturate overdose. She was fifty-five. Edith was described as a very beautiful woman, tall and statuesque, stately and dignified in bearing but with a lively sense of humor and an easy laugh. Barbiturates were readily prescribed in the 1940s as a sleep aid and to treat anxiety, and unfortunately many patients became unwittingly addicted. In his grief, Kurt leaned on Jane, which brought them even closer.

In June, Jane graduated from Swarthmore with high honors and was elected to Phi Beta Kappa. She was also awarded a prize for having the best personal library of any graduating student; she had an extensive collection of Russian literature, volumes of poetry, and all of Shakespeare's works. In late summer, Jane moved to Washington, D.C., to begin a job as a clerk analyst in the counterintelligence branch of the Office of Strategic Services

(OSS), the predecessor of the CIA. Jane did secretive work as a research assistant, specializing in the Far East while also studying Russian at George Washington University.

By September, Kurt was packing to go overseas with the rest of the 106th Division. Fifteen thousand soldiers were being sent to relieve the 2nd Division at the front in Belgium.

On October 17, Kurt set sail from Manhattan on the *Queen Elizabeth* and arrived in Cheltenham, England, two weeks later. On December 6, the 106th Division crossed the English Channel, waded ashore at Le Havre, France, and drove into Belgium. Ten days later, on December 16, Kurt's division was swept into the Battle of the Bulge, during which he was taken prisoner of war along with 7,000 others and marched hundreds of miles into Germany. On December 21, Kurt's family was notified that he was missing in action.

Pfc. Kurt Vonnegut
D-2, A.S.T.P. 4431
TENN. U., KNOXVILLE, TENN.

Free

KNOXVILLE
MAR 13
10³⁰ PM
1944
TENN.

JANE M. COX
SWARTHMORE COLLEGE
SWARTHMORE, PA.

Through mighty fights and awful plights
And fever's dread delirium —
My only need, my only creed,
Is to clean my teeth with
Irium

USN
T.B.T

Dear Woofy:

Maybe you've mailed me some biting and terribly just rebuttle to my last inane outburst from Knoxville — I don't know. I've moved so often since that I've not got a letter for a couple of weeks. Well, no matter.

I'm in Battallion Intelligence now, in the 106th Division, in a staging area — Camp Atterbury. I got home last week-end and saw Riah and Thos. H. at the Player's Club dance. They were very pleasant, seeming to be having a near-ecstatic time. They said Hairbreadth Harry had planned to be at the dance but had, at the last minute, been unable to attend — bombing U-boats in the Wabash I should imagine. Your family was radiant in giving me the impression that Bloody Bruce is something not far removed from a gentile Jesus. I shall seek him out once more if I can get another pass.

I feel one helluva lot better now that I'm back with combat troops. The 106th has completed it's training, having just come from Tennessee maneuvers in which it was judged the best. We've just been given overseas physicals (I passed) and furloughs are being given out (I'm not eligible).

My new job is to cover my face and hands with soot and crawl into enemy lines to see what in hell they've got. This isn't dramatizing my position — I've been given a job and that's it. There are seven of us in the battallion; we work singly or in pairs. It is a job so completely foreign to my nature that I'm getting a pleasurable tic out of anticipating doing it under the nose of the enemy — a sunburst of new sensations — possibly you understand.

I may still be here when and if you come home in June or before. I hope to see you, though the motive and mission are obscure. In any event, Woofy, please write.

Love,

Kurt —

4 - 19 - 44

Dear Woofy:

I like you. I think I like you more than anyone else in the world; you tell me what I want to hear; you ask me questions I love to answer. I like the letter I got today.

I like your fiendish curiosity. If you were to say, "All right, let's get married in 1945?" When you posed the question you surely realized what a Delphic question it was: 1946, 1947, or 1948 for that matter. I may be dead before the war ends. People, even people you know quite well, do get killed. Apparently ours is not an undeniable passion, like Jim's and Allie's, perhaps, that tells us to be greedily in love; to take great mouthfulls of everything on the banquet-board before us. It was once. Tell me, would you ~~be it~~ enjoy living with me, sleeping with me, leading a carnival life? Do you ever think about it and think it would be good? Carnival life! I'll explain:-sideshow after sideshow—half-truths, colorfully

84

displayed,—the net effects of our roccoco environments and educations; with intermittent Ferris wheels and Lindy Loops,—occasional binges and my chasing you naked all over the bedroom. Would you like that, Woofy? Do you think it's a thing we should have, a thing you would bitterly regret having missed were I killed? Do you love me? That's important.

Or possibly you assume that the war will be over in 1945. I am once more a civilian, unscathed. Were you to accept my hypothetical proposal I would suffer minor shock — coming face to face with the full-blown fruit of years of playful effort would have that effect. Once aclimated to the astonishing situation I've got myself into I would be both delighted and proud — a world beater, I think. If, instead of giving me a riddle, you had said, "Let's get married in 1945" I would have replied, "Good idea, Woofy. We will be happy. If I am here in 1945 we'll do it."

Maybe, when and if you come home soon, Kendall and I will meet. I'll not seek him out. Week-ends are too short. The general conception of polygamy is one man with two or more wives. I can't see it any other way.

Jimmy Adams wrote that he will try to get me into the Public Relations Office of the European Theater of War. That's his current station — in England. It all hinges on the 100th Division's releasing me. I don't think they will. Dear, sweet Jesus I hope it comes through.

Ho, Woofy, I'm not really a scientist but rather a passionate and comprehending fan of science. It's like the lament, "I sing so sweet and it comes out so sour." That's about the size of it. I know a ~~lot~~ lot of fascinating little things like why the wind blows, why things mildew in damp places, how long it will take for a stone to fall from the top to the bottom of the Grand Canyon, how to hold my breath for three minutes, why steel bridges are built the way they are, that sperm travels only upward etc. I like being able to explain things. I can explain a lot.

Allie will have her baby in about six weeks. If you want to have a baby please come home and let it be mine. I asked first.

About revolutionizing education — just what is your plan — universal Orchard School? You ommitted mention of just what changes do you have in mind? Yes, I should say you could influence young minds — surely. You're just the person, Woofy, to do that. That you should want to do this — dabble or wreak in education, that is — comes as a surprise to me, but upon reflection is wonderfully sound. Tell me your ideas and I'll try to criticize them.

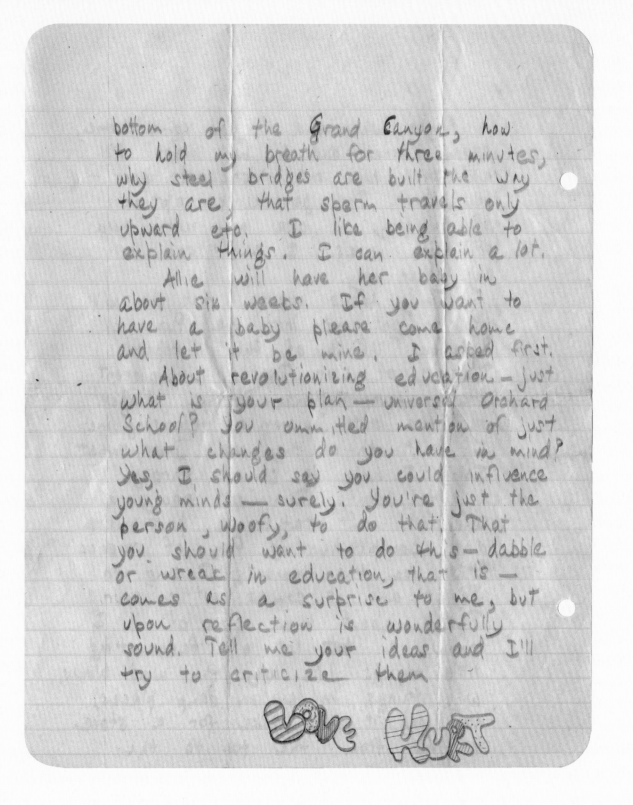

LOVE HURT

5.3.44

Dear Woofy:

When I consider how my love is spent
e're half my days in this dark world and
wide I wonder why you - (that person in whose
being so much of my love has been spent) - are
not here with me to relish and interpret in
terms of the nobility and full-bodied lush justice
of life this omnipotent warm Spring day.
Jane, Darling, at this moment, as I write, you are
being loved so much that my heart is nearly
bursting. That love is inbred, a thing I can't
deny and which, under the compunction of an uninhibited and completely naked and shapely Proserpine
I have given free rein. At a full run,
dearest, with the wind rushing past my ears,
with the hot sun beating down on my bare
head, with clouds of dust rolling behind, I love
you, Jane.

I shan't be here when you return.
But in your heart know this — I've loved you
with more violence and passion than riot or
rebellion. You've been loved well this lovely
Spring day.

Kurt —

Pfc Kurt Vonnegut 12102964
HQ. Co., 2ND BN., 423 INF
A.P.O. 443, CAMP ATTERBURY,

INDIANAPOLIS, IND.
MAY 9
6:30 PM
1944

JANE MARIE COX

SWARTHMORE   COLLEGE

SWARTHMORE, PA.

5·8·44

Dear Woofy:

Someone said that there are three kinds of lies: little white lies, big lies, and statistics. Here are a few statistics, built on the miserable fact that we have been together nine hours out of a little more than a year.

At that rate we have been together one hour out of every thousand hours —

One day out of every three years —

One month out of a lifetime or about half that part of your life dedicated to brushing your teeth —

And were we to be together for what remains of our lives (our prewar birthright) we would have to be born in 50 000 B.C., the Early Stone Age, when man first used fire and was learning to chip crude weapons from flint, before he moved into caves!

ALL OF THIS IS VERY SAD AND WILL DOUBTLESS BECOME MUCH WORSE.

5-30.44

Dear Woofy:

Your warm letter is beside me now.

Allie and I found mother curled up as if asleep. There was no distortion — nothing grotesque. In the simplest, the legendary way, mother died. Absolute normalcy: birth, a few years, and then death.

Grief over a death is a selfish thing and the magnitude of the genuine grief is in a way a monument to the deceased. I still need my mother terribly, Woofy. It is a

source of self-damnation
that I should have been
such a prosaic adolescent,
vociferously denying that
mother was still the reservoir
of my strength. These things
I should have said to my
mother I have left unsaid.
That is the melancholy and
haunting thought. What is this
thing that makes people deny
full and frequent expression
of love and devotion? My
train of thought becomes
less commonplace and maudlin
in the light of a thing I
may have intimated to you:
mother was -(as a result of
a cruelly severe menopause) - at

times completely irrational.
Your experience with such
matters was perhaps more sustained
than mine but we've both
been on the same rack
— and it is an unbelievably
excruciating rack. There-in
lies a bond of which you
may not have been consc-
ious. While on that rack
my reactions were frequently
more human than compassion-
ate. Tolerance . tolerance . tolerance.
I must be tolerant. I must
try to understand. The
variations in human nature
are degrees of illness. I've
got to remember that. Please

never mention to anyone
what I've just said. It
cried out to be told. Words
between us are uninhibited
and for such a relationship
I am grateful.

It is rather for us, the
living, to be here dedicated—:
and dedicated we are, Bernard,
Alice and Kay, to those elements
of our mother which were
her birthright: complete and
unselfish devotion to her
family; morality; inflexible sense
of fair play; childlike love
for all things alive. I see
now the what and why of
my being. Mother is dead. I
can't tell her what I know.

I need someone to tell
me big, wonderful lies about
myself — someone to be deeply
concerned about me — I want to
feel that someone is watching
my every move and giving
very much of a damn — I
want a deep and boundless
love that I can brashly
abuse and be forgiven for
it. These playthings were
mine two weeks ago. I
cried for a very long time.

If I'm not mistaken, you
will graduate around June 27.
Very nicely done, Woofy — as
well as is possible I
should suppose. The question

now rises in my mind: what
manner of person are you
— emerging from your cocoon?
What are your plans? Public
Relations in England says they
will take me but I must
first get over there. I've
pulled wires to that end. How
long it will take me I've
no idea. You'll be home in late
June or early July, I guess.
● My hope is that we'll see
each other at that time.
There's nothing I want more.
Allie's baby is due at
any minute. Life goes on and
on and on for billions of
years until the Sun burns up
— then it and immortality die. Love, Kurt

6 · 16 · 44

Dear Woofy:

    In that you have completed sixteen years of the best education this country has to offer, and in that you have done the best possible work during each of those sixteen years, and in that my own education has been punctuated with much gnashing of teeth and chagrin, I take awed note of your graduation.

    My garbled college education to date has been, from a humanistic standpoint, shallow and insipid at best. Yours has been neither of those, certainly. "A cultivated heart and a disciplined mind are elements of power."—Caleb Mills, naturally. Those elements are yours now, I should suppose. But, upon reflection, those elements have, for the few years during which I've known you, been evident potentialities. A thing to which I look foreward is the precipitation of all things floating about inside of you—impulses, passions, inhibitions—into tangible, sparkling, multicolored crystals.

It must be a pretty rough experience to be suddenly pronounced complete

and expelled into the world.
I haven't had that happen
to me as yet. Methinks
that after the war I'll
hedge around a little longer
by going to the University
of Chicago Law School.
    I hope to see you in
fifteen more days and nights.
At that time I'll congratulate
the hell out of you.

            Love —

                KURT

July 22-1944

Dear Woofy:

    If you haven't already seen this it will astonish the hell out of you. It did me. This is a masterfully compiled, unbelievable coincidence — nothing more. But isn't it wonderfully convincing?

    Please save it for me as it's my only copy. Save me a date this coming Saturday if you possibly can or are so inclined.

Love,
Kurt

	CHURCHILL	HITLER	ROOSEVELT	IL DUCE	STALIN	TOJO
YEAR BORN	1874	1889	1882	1883	1879	1884
AGE	70	55	62	61	65	60
TOOK OFFICE	1940	1933	1933	1922	1924	1941
YEARS IN SERVICE	4	11	11	22	20	3
TOTAL	3888	3888	3888	3888	3888	3888

END OF THE WAR: $\frac{1}{2}$ OF 3888 = 1944

$\frac{1}{2}$ OF 1944 = 972 = 9 MONTHS, 7 DAYS, 2 P.M.

TO FIND THE SUPREME RULER TAKE FIRST LETTER OF EACH NAME

CHRIST

August 7-1944

Dearest Woofy —:

Time alone is without limits.
All other things can endure
only a fragment of eternity: necessarily
with a beginning, a middle and
an end. We have begun. Beyond
that the timetable is stupid and
meaningless. That may explain the
dismal void that besets me
today: an insistant, foolish melancholy
gremlin. I didn't get to talk to
you sunday, Woofy; to say how
much I loved you the night
before; to say I looked foreward
to being with you in another
six days and to say good-bye
until then.

Jane, darling, dammit — you are
such a sensationally 'attractive'
little girl to me that I can't

102

POST CARD

CASTLE BARN — ROAD 67 — INDIANAPOLIS, IND.

FIRST
CLASS
MAIL

PLACE
3 CENT
STAMP
HERE

DARLING —
  THERE'S ENOUGH
LOVE FOR YOU IN MY
HEART AT THIS MOMENT
TO LAST THE
GODDAMN NORMAL
PERSON A LIFETIME. KOOKI

JANE M. COX

96TH + N. COLLEGE

INDIANAPOLIS, IND

help but love you.
Yin and Yan are too
wonderfully smooth on all surfaces
to call to mind any persons
I've known—least of all, us.
The union of most human patterns
results in something less symmetrical
than a circle. But, Jane, darling
dammit, we're every bit as
Euclidian as Yin and Yan——:
πr^2 is our area and $2\pi r$
is our circumference.
Much much much
love—

KURT

23 August 44

Darling Woofy:

Wouldst thou wert here, my love, for this mellow eventide the antique intellect of some lyrical ancestor has risen to flood my sleepy head with quaint love melodies. Dear sweet lady— I love thee. Thou art as my heart, a pulsating within me, throbbing through the hot sunlit day; beating softly through the black velvet of night. Were it to stop my body would die and decay. My love for thee is as my soul, bounded by the universe, that imperishible shadow of me that will make my loves and

105

hater known though my
flesh be ashes. Thou art
of all lovely things on
earth dearest to me.

...And that's no damned
joke, Jane, darling: nothing
has ever meant so much
to me as you. Being away
from you makes me want
to cry like a lost little
boy. I want the blessed
warmth of you. Fantastic
phantasmagoria — I love
love love you.

Kurt —

September 17, 1944

Dear Woofy:

Did it ever occur to you that I am mildly concerned over whether you are with or without child? Please say something, sweet Jane Marie. Paternity is small apples stacked up against motherhood, I admit, but I do feel implicated in my minor capacity. So drop me a post-card with either YES or NO on it: YES meaning, "I am going to have a baby—your baby"; NO meaning, "I'm not going to have a baby—your baby."

I'm not meaning to be sarcastic, Woofy, honest. And this isn't a reprimand for your not having written to me. It wouldn't and wont surprise

me never to hear from you
again. I'll say this—you are
fortunate in being able to
forget things we've said and
done together—not so very
long ago. It must make
you an admirably efficient
(and I swear I'm not
meaning to be satirical—
neither that nor bitter) person
to have about. That in
contrast to myself whose moony
efficiency hardly justifies this
lean and lanky bulk. I never
could be busy enough (I have
been in several industrious
situations, you'll admit) not to
indulge myself in the vanity of
being in love with you.
        Of course, my more recently

enforced tasks have been dismal
affairs. This may be a case
of the grass being greener on
the other side of the fence.
But that's where the proverb
falls flat, because, you, see,
dear heart, I know for a
fact that the grass is
greener, much greener, on the
other side. It's green as
emeralds, has a texture like a
blanket, a fragrance like gardenias.
I remember. You don't.

Woman — you, at least — seem
to be like that: not mean, not
perfidious, not deceitful but
instantaniously passionate,
irrational, at full flood tide, hot,
turgid with florid meaning —

4

Then, aloof, practical, ebbed
and placid, cold, flat as
last night's beer. You can't
help being that way, darling,
any more than a thermometer
can help rising in a heat
wave. Men are like street cars
—(if you miss one, another
will be along in ten minutes)—
you're like thermometers and
barometers. There's not much
sense to my getting mad about
it, is there? Especially since,
besides not being to help yourself,
you are probably right — and
I'm implicitly wrong. Wrong:
poetic license as opposed to
sentiments in keeping with the
times; pursuit of happiness as

opposed to patriotism; hoosier
as opposed to world citizen;
love as opposed to industry;
Ben Franklin stove as opposed
to Schwitzer-Cummins Stoker;
enchantment as opposed to
reality; reality as opposed to
enchantment; me as opposed to
you. Regretable and pathetic
as this may strike you, lovely,
bear in mind that I can't
help being and doing what I
do any more than you can.
Me as opposed to you; memory
as opposed to forgetfulness.
Amnesia is a last-ditch defense
mechanism. Against what, I don't
know. Amnesia is your way out;
vivid recollection is mine. I

recall the warmth of your
cheek and breath; the sound
of your laugh and what
made you laugh; the heavenly
things you've said and implied.
You don't, you can't remember.
I guess you don't want to
—either drunk or caught in
the splendid spirit of love-making.
            We're leaving Atterbury
for P.O.E. on October 5th.
I shall probably be 22
before going overseas. I
may see you soon.

Love —

Kurt

AIR MAIL

INDIANAPOLIS.IND.
AUG 4
1-PM
1945

Insufficient Postage for Air Mail

UNITED STATES POSTAGE
3 CENTS 3

Jane   Marie   Cox
3752   W.   Street,   N.W.
Washington,   D.C.

Retention's Pretention

...Passion's the Fashion

October 26. 1944

Dear Woofy:

Either you've given me the
axe or enemy submarines
are concentrating on mail
boats. I haven't had
a sweet nothing from you
for a couple of months.

I'm overseas, dear heart,
in a land full of poetic
references which the censor
wont let me make. The
same may be said for caustic
comment.

Of all the letters I've
written to you (How many; hundreds?)
not one has included a sound
piece of information. That policy
will continue in force: What
I say in letters to you is

particularly no one's business.
Sometimes I think it's
none of your business. You
too?

Just to keep you up
to date on the situation;
I love you more than
anything else in the world.
Hasn't changed much since the
summer of 1940 when you
nosed out my dog, has it? I've
plenty of time to think now.
For all practical purposes I'm
still 20 years old. In the
pursuit of happiness I doubt
if I've maintained my status
of 1942. In fact, the only thing
I've seriously pursued since is you.

"Hacker, hacker, hacker—" I should have pawned everything I owned in order to go with you on the Jeffersonian. You see, Woofy, I actually believed that I could bamboozle you into marrying me before I left. I didn't, and, contrary to the attitudes of more rational folks, I'm bitterly sorry you didn't.

J.T. Alburger wrote to tell me SEMPER CONFUSIS that he's in limited service — doomed to live on the West Coast with his wife until the war is over. Jeff is flying bombers etc. in the states in the Ferry Command.

He's making $225 per month
plus $7 per day for every
day he's away from his
Detroit base. Buck is a
rifleman in Florida — Private
in the Infantry. Skip, I
surmise, is still in France.
Hite is resigned to placid
4-F-dom in a quiet clerical
job. The fortunes of war
are beyond my comprehension
or sympathy. Those that
draw conclusions from a man's
war record are God-damned
fools.

    If I come home in
fairly decent condition please
marry me, Woofy. I'll make

you sensationally happy and
have a fair time out of
it for myself. There are
a million wonderful reasons
why it would work—one
of which is financial.
   Well, nuts—I probably
shan't be back. But if
I'm not, I'll raise spiritual
hell with your ouija board.

LOVE

Kurt II

Dearest Jane, darling....

Things are back to normal. They've got to be back to normal. Your loving me, or having loved me, is the most generous gift God ever gave me.

I've never been so full of love for you as I am this Sunday morning. This war will last for five years at the least. Many of us will die. Look about you: what friends of ours will die? --George? Benny? Victor? Buck? Cornell will soon be wrecked; D.U. will be shuttered. My chances for finishing college are slim. My chances for fullfilling any of my big dreams are slowly fading--with one exception, the biggest dream. The one happiness I look foreward to is living with you, having children by you. Darling, I love you.

This is a destitute, hating, bleeding world. Our lifetime will be a warped one. We may be married a great deal sooner than we first dared to hope for. Body and soul, darling, I want you.

Please see me Sunday night, December 21st.

+ + + + + + +

(KURT)

1945:
DRESDEN FIREBOMBING
AND COMING HOME

FOR SIX MONTHS, JANE DID NOT KNOW IF KURT WAS DEAD OR ALIVE. She had become good friends with Kurt's sister, Allie, by this time, and the two women stayed in close contact after he was reported missing in action.

During this period of silence, Kurt was one of 150 POWs taken by train to Dresden. On February 13 and 14, 1945, Dresden was firebombed by the British and United States Air Forces, killing between 35,000 and 135,000 people in twenty-four hours. The real figure will almost certainly never be known, as there were so many refugees in the city at the time. For the next two months, Kurt was put to work by the Germans, clearing rubble and collecting corpses for huge funeral pyres. By mid-April, the war was showing signs of ending, and on April 13, German troops marched their prisoners out of Dresden to the Czech border over the course of two days and abandoned them there. By May, Kurt was delivered to the POW repatriation center at Camp Lucky Strike in Havre, Le France.

Finally, Kurt was able to write home and tell his family that he was safe and what had happened to him. They then shared the news with Jane. He even came up with his dream meal for his homecoming.

From:

To: KURT VONNEGUT
WILLIAMS CREEK
INDIANAPOLIS, IND.

PFC. K. VONNEGUT, JR.
12102964 U.S. ARMY

PAGE ONE

[CENSOR'S STAMP]   See Instruction No. 2   (Sender's complete address above)

DEAR PEOPLE:
    I'M TOLD THAT YOU WERE PROBABLY NEVER INFORMED
THAT I WAS ANYTHING OTHER THAN "MISSING IN ACTION."
CHANCES ARE THAT YOU ALSO FAILED TO RECEIVE ANY
OF THE LETTERS I WROTE FROM GERMANY. THAT
LEAVES ME A LOT OF EXPLAINING TO DO — IN PRECIS:
    I'VE BEEN A PRISONER OF WAR SINCE DECEMBER
19TH, 1944 WHEN OUR DIVISION WAS CUT TO RIBBONS
BY HITLER'S LAST DESPERATE THRUST THROUGH LUXEMBURG
AND BELGIUM. SEVEN FANATICAL PANZER DIVISIONS HIT US
AND CUT US OFF FROM THE REST OF HODGES' FIRST
ARMY. THE OTHER AMERICAN DIVISIONS ON OUR FLANKS
MANAGED TO PULL OUT: WE WERE OBLIGED TO STAY
AND FIGHT. BAYONETS AREN'T MUCH GOOD AGAINST
TANKS: OUR AMMUNITION, FOOD AND MEDICAL SUPPLIES
GAVE OUT AND OUR CASUALTIES OUTNUMBERED THOSE
WHO COULD STILL FIGHT — SO WE GAVE UP. THE
106TH GOT A PRESIDENTIAL CITATION AND SOME BRITISH
DECORATION FROM MONTGOMERY FOR IT, I'M TOLD, BUT
I'LL BE DAMNED IF IT WAS WORTH IT. I WAS
ONE OF THE FEW WHO WEREN'T WOUNDED. FOR THAT
MUCH THANK GOD.

HAVE YOU FILLED IN COMPLETE
ADDRESS AT TOP?

REPLY BY
V···MAIL

HAVE YOU FILLED IN COMPLETE
ADDRESS AT TOP?

To: KURT VONNEGUT
WILLIAMS CREEK
INDIANAPOLIS, IND.

From:
PFC K. VONNEGUT, JR.
12102964 U.S. ARMY
PAGE TWO

(CENSOR'S STAMP)   See Instruction No. 2   (Sender's complete address above)

. WELL, THE SUPERMEN MARCHED US, WITHOUT FOOD, WATER
OR SLEEP TO LIMBERG, A DISTANCE OF ABOUT SIXTY MILES,
I THINK, WHERE WE WERE LOADED AND LOCKED UP, SIXTY
MEN TO EACH SMALL, UNVENTILATED, UNHEATED BOX CAR.
THERE WERE NO SANITARY ACCOMODATIONS — THE FLOORS
WERE COVERED WITH FRESH COW DUNG. THERE WASN'T
ROOM FOR ALL OF US TO LIE DOWN. HALF SLEPT
WHILE THE OTHER HALF STOOD. WE SPENT SEVERAL
DAYS, INCLUDING CHRISTMAS ON THAT LIMBERG SIDING. ON
CHRISTMAS EVE THE ROYAL AIR FORCE BOMBED AND
STRAFED OUR UNMARKED TRAIN. THEY KILLED ABOUT
ONE-HUNDRED-AND-FIFTY OF US. WE GOT A LITTLE WATER
CHRISTMAS DAY AND MOVED SLOWLY ACROSS GERMANY TO
A LARGE P.O.W. CAMP IN MÜHLBURG, SOUTH OF BERLIN.
WE WERE RELEASED FROM THE BOX CARS ON NEW YEAR'S
DAY. THE GERMANS HERDED US THROUGH SCALDING
DELOUSING SHOWERS. MANY MEN DIED FROM SHOCK IN
THE SHOWERS AFTER TEN DAYS OF STARVATION, THIRST
AND EXPOSURE. BUT I DIDN'T.
          UNDER THE GENEVA CONVENTION, OFFICERS AND
NON-COMMISSIONED OFFICERS ARE NOT OBLIGED TO

HAVE YOU FILLED IN COMPLETE
ADDRESS AT TOP?

REPLY BY
V----MAIL

HAVE YOU FILLED IN COMPLETE
ADDRESS AT TOP?

22

From:

To: KURT VONNEGUT
WILLIAMS CREEK
INDIANAPOLIS, IND.

PFC. K. VONNEGUT, JR.
12102964 U.S. ARMY
PAGE THREE

...ICE WHEN TAKEN PRISONER. I AM, AS YOU KNOW,
A PRIVATE. ONE-HUNDRED-AND-FIFTY. SUCH MINOR BEINGS
ARE SHIPPED TO A DRESDEN WORK CAMP ON
JANUARY 10TH. I WAS THEIR LEADER BY VIRTUE OF
THE LITTLE GERMAN I SPOKE. IT WAS OUR MISFORTUNE
TO HAVE SADISTIC AND FANATICAL GUARDS. WE
WERE REFUSED MEDICAL ATTENTION and CLOTHING: WE WERE
GIVEN LONG HOURS AT EXTREMELY HARD LABOR.
OUR FOOD RATION WAS TWO-HUNDRED-AND-FIFTY GRAMS
OF BLACK BREAD AND ONE PINT OF UNSEASONED
POTATO SOUP EACH DAY. AFTER DESPERATELY
TRYING TO IMPROVE OUR SITUATION FOR TWO
MONTHS AND HAVING BEEN MET WITH BLAND
SMILES I TOLD THE GUARDS JUST WHAT I WAS
GOING TO DO TO THEM WHEN THE RUSSIANS
CAME. THEY BEAT ME UP A LITTLE. I WAS
FIRED AS GROUP LEADER. BEATINGS WERE VERY
SMALL TIME — ONE BOY STARVED TO DEATH AND
THE SS TROOPS SHOT TWO FOR STEALING FOOD.
ON ABOUT FEBRUARY 14TH THE AMERICANS CAME
OVER, FOLLOWED BY THE RAF. THEIR COMBINED

From:

To: KURT VONNEGUT
WILLIAMS CREEK
INDIANAPOLIS, IND.

PFC. K. VONNEGUT
12102964, U.S.A.

PAGE FOUR

(CENSOR'S STAMP)   See Instruction No. 2   (Sender's complete address abo

KILLED 250,000 PEOPLE IN TWENTY-FOU HOURS AND DESTROYED ALL OF DRESDEN—POSSIB. THE WORLD'S MOST BEAUTIFUL CITY. BUT NOT ME.

AFTER THAT WE WERE PUT TO WORK CARRYIN CORPSES FROM AIR-RAID SHELTERS: WOMEN, CHILDREN OLD MEN: DEAD FROM CONCUSSION, FIRE OR SUFFOC CIVILIANS CURSED US AND THREW ROCKS AS WE CARRIED BODIES TO HUGE FUNERAL PYRES IN THE CITY.

WHEN GENERAL PATON TOOK LEIPZIG WE WERE EVACUATED ON FOOT TO HELLEXISDORF ON THE SAXONY-CZECHOSLOVAKIAN BORDER. THERE WE REMAIN UNTIL THE WAR ENDED. OUR GUARDS DESERTED ON THAT HAPPY DAY THE RUSSIANS WERE INTE ON MOPPING UP ISOLATED OUTLAW RESISTANCE OUR SECTOR. THEIR PLANES (P-39's) STRAFED AN BOMBED US, KILLING FOURTEEN. BUT NOT ME.

EIGHT IF US STOLE A TEAM AND WAGON. WE TRAVELED AND LOOTED OUR WAY THROUGH

HAVE YOU FILLED IN COMPLETE ADDRESS AT TOP?

REPLY BY
V---MAIL

HAVE YOU FILLED IN COMPLE ADDRESS AT TOP?

22

In plain letters in the pane below, and your return address in the space provided on ... dark ink, or dark pencil. Faint or small writing is not suitable for photographing.

To:
KURT VONNEGUT
WILLIAMS CREEK
INDIANAPOLIS, IND.

See Instruction No. 2

From:
Pfc. K. VONNEGUT, JR.
12102964 U.S. ARMY
PAGE FIVE

(Sender's complete address above)

SUDETENLAND AND SAXONY FOR EIGHT DAYS, LIVING
LIKE KINGS. THE RUSSIANS ARE CRAZY ABOUT ⑤
AMERICANS. THE RUSSIANS PICKED US UP IN
DRESDEN. WE RODE FROM THERE TO THE
AMERICAN LINES AT HALLE IN LEND-LEASE FORD
TRUCKS. WE'VE SINCE BEEN FLOWN TO
LE HAVRE.

I'M WRITING FROM A RED CROSS CLUB IN
THE LE HAVRE P.O.W. REPATRIATION CAMP. I'M
BEING WONDERFULLY WELL FED AND ENTERTAINED.
THE STATE-BOUND SHIPS ARE JAMMED, NATURALLY,
SO I'LL HAVE TO BE PATIENT. I HOPE TO
BE HOME IN A MONTH. ONCE HOME I'LL
BE GIVEN TWENTY-ONE DAYS RECUPERATION AT
ATTERBURY ABOUT $600 BACK PAY AND —GET THIS—
SIXTY (0) DAYS FURLOUGH!

I'VE TOO DAMNED MUCH TO SAY. THE
REST WILL HAVE TO WAIT. I CAN'T RECEIVE
MAIL HERE SO DON'T WRITE.

MAY 29, 1945

LOVE

Kurt Jr.

HAVE YOU FILLED IN COMPLETE
ADDRESS AT TOP?

REPLY BY
V····MAIL

HAVE YOU FILLED IN COMPLETE
ADDRESS AT TOP?

Signal Corps, United States Army

Received at

NR 3826

KURT VONNEGUT
RIDGE ROAD,
WILLIAMS CREEK INDIANAPOLIS IND.

IN GOOD HANDS HEALTH AND SPIRITS BE HOME BY
BOAT SOON GOD IS MY CHUM.

Recd May 31 '45

KURT VONNEGUT JR 12102964

From:

To: KURT VONNEGUT
WILLIAMS CREEK
INDIANAPOLIS, IND.
U.S.A

PFC. K. VONNEGUT, JR
12102964 - R.A.M.P.
U.S. ARMY - FRANCE

(CENSOR'S STAMP)

See Instruction No. 2

(Sender's complete address above)

DEAR FAMILY:

MY LAST LETTER WAS UNNECCESSARILY MORBID, I FEAR. A PERPETUALLY TIGHT BELLY HAS PRETTY WELL OBLITERATED RECOLLECTIONS OF WHAT HAPPENED TO ME IN GERMANY—: EVERY TIME MY MEMORY PEAKS UP I CALL IT A GODDAMN LIAR.

BESIDES, THE FUTURE IS MORE INTERESTING. WHAT THAT FUTURE WILL, BEYOND A BOAT TRIP HOME IN A FEW (?) WEEKS AND TWO MONTHS OF FURLOUGH, I DON'T KNOW. THERE ARE TOO MANY UNANSWERED QUESTIONS: QUESTIONS THAT MUST REMAIN UNANSWERED UNTIL I REACH HOME, BY VIRTUE OF MY NOT BEING ABLE TO RECEIVE MAIL HERE. IS ALL WELL AT HOME? WHO IS HOME? WHERE IS HOME? ~~~~~~~ IS WOOFY ENGAGED OR MARRIED? WILL SHE MARRY ME? WILL I BE SENT TO THE PACIFIC? IF SO, IN WHAT CAPACITY? THE ANSWERS TO THE LAST TWO ARE, I'M AFRAID, RESPECTIVELY YES, YOU POOR FISH, AND INFANTRYMAN!— THAT IS, UNLESS I PULL SOME WIRES DURING MY FURLOUGH.

IDEALLY, THIS IS THE WAY I SHOULD LIKE THINGS TO WORK: DURING MY FURLOUGH I WOULD WORK AS A REPORTER ON ONE OF THE INDIANAPOLIS PAPERS — THAT, SIMULTANIOUS WITH THE STUDY AND PERFECTION OF GERMAN AND THE REBUILDING OF MY PHYSICAL SELF THROUGH EXERCISE. THIS SOBER AND WELL-MEANING PLAN MAY BE LIQUIDATED AT A MOMENT'S NOTICE IN FAVOR OF A HONEYMOON, PROVIDING I LOVE WOOFY AND WOOFY LOVES ME,—WHICH REMAINS TO BE VERIFIED.

(MORE)

To: KURT VONNEGUT
WILLIAMS CREEK
INDIANAPOLIS, IND.
U.S.A.

From:
PFC. KURT VONNEGUT JR.
2102964 - R.A.M.P.
U.S. ARMY - FRANCE

(CENSOR'S STAMP)   See Instruction No. 2   (Sender's complete address above)

I FIND THAT I HAVEN'T A CHANCE FOR DISCHARGE
UNDER THE POINT DISCHARGE SYSTEM 85 POINTS ARE
REQUIRED. I HAVE SOMETHING LIKE 43. I'M DAMNED
IF I WANT ANY MORE OF THIS INFANTRY PRIVATE DEAL.
WHAT I WOULD LIKE TO DO IS TO RETURN TO
GERMANY AND USE MY SPEAKING ABILITY AND ROCK
BOTTOM KNOWLEDGE OF THE PEOPLE TO ADVANTAGE —
OR, BETTER STILL, LAND A DECENT JOB IN THE
STATES. I DUNNO — WE'LL HAVE TO SEE.
    I'VE ONLY A VAGUE IDEA WHEN I'LL BE HOME.
SHIPPING IS HOPELESSLY CROWDED AND I AM ONE
OF THE LAST P.O.W.'S TO ARRIVE HERE [CAMP
LUCKY STRIKE, NEAR LE HAVRE]. VERY LATE IN JUNE
OR SOMETIME IN JULY — SORRY, THAT'S THE BEST I
CAN DO.

            MUCH LOVE

                    KURT-JR.

From:

To: KURT VONNEGUT, SR.
RIDGE ROAD, WILLIAMS CREEK
INDIANAPOLIS, INDIANA
U.S.A

PFC. KURT VONNEGUT, JR
12102964
UNITED STATES ARMY
GERMANY

(CENSOR'S STAMP)　　See Instruction No. 2　　(Sender's complete address above)

MAY 18, 1945

DEAR PEOPLE:

IT IS A SOURCE OF GREAT DELIGHT TO BE ABLE TO ANNOUNCE THAT YOU WILL SHORTLY RECEIVE A SPLENDID RELIC OF WORLD WAR II WITH WHICH YOU MAY DECORATE YOUR HEARTH —— NAMELY ME IN AN EXCELLENT STATE OF PRESERVATION. YOU MAY WELL SAY "HUZZAH!" FOR THIS PRODIGAL PRINCELING HAS SURVIVED THE COMBINED ORDEALS OF JOB AND THE PROVERBIAL PAPERHANGER WITH PILES DURING THESE HISTORY-TURGID SIX MONTHS JUST ELAPSED. PRAISE JESUS, OUR GROUP WAS HELD PRISONER BY THE GERMANS UNTIL THE VERY END WHEN OUR GUARDS LEFT US, THEIR RIFLES AND NATIONAL SOCIALISM IN FAVOR OF COMMUNISM WHICH IS ENJOYING GREAT POPULARITY IN OUR PART OF THE COUNTRY. EIGHT OF US HAVE BEEN TOURING GERMANY BY HORSE AND WAGON SINCE V-DAY, TRYING TO LOCATE SOMEONE WHO WASN'T TOO BUSY TO LIBERATE US. WE SUCCEEDED ONLY TWO DAYS AGO. THE DOPE HERE IS THAT WE'LL BE FLOWN HOME SHORTLY. I'M A SHADOW OF MY FORMER SHADOW BECAUSE THE BASTARDS TRIED TO STARVE ME TO DEATH BUT THEIR TIME RAN OUT BEFORE MINE. IT WILL SOON BE YOUR MAUDLIN DUTY TO SET GOODIES BEFORE ME THAT I MAY ONCE MORE BE MY MERRY, CURLY-TOPPED, LITTLE-OL'-BUTTERBALL SELF.

LOVE - KURT II

HAVE YOU FILLED IN COMPLETE ADDRESS AT TOP?

V-MAIL

HAVE YOU FILLED IN COMPLETE ADDRESS AT TOP?

DRY MARTINI
CAVIAR AND CRACKED WHOLE WHEAT CRACKERS

SHRIMP COCKTAIL WITH TOMATO AND HORSERADISH SAUCE

CLAM CHOWDER
OYSTER CRACKERS

WHOLE BAKED CHICKEN WITH OYSTER DRESSING
SAUTERN

MASHED POTATOES WITH GIBLET GRAVY
CREAMED ASPARAGUS TIPS
CANDIED SWEET POTATOES
FRIED TOMATOES AND CRACKER CRUMBS
OLIVES, SWEET PICKLES, CELERY, PICKLED ONIONS
COTTAGE CHEESE AND PINEAPPLE SALAD WITH MAYONNAISE

PARKERHOUSE ROLLS, CORN BREAD
BUTTER, HONEY, GRAPE JELLY

STRAWBERRY SHORTCAKE WITH WHIPPED CREAM

CAFE AU LAIT
SALTINES AND LIMBERGER CHEESE

TOLLHOUSE COOKIES, MIXED NUTS, CHOCOLATE BUDS

CHERRY BRANDY
CORONA CORONA CIGAR

K. VONNEGUT, JR

HELLENDORF, SAXONY, GERMANY

1945

✝

AMERICAN RED CROSS

DEAR ANGELFACE:

As I recall, you and I were quite warm friends when last together about eight months ago——: you should, therefore, derive some small pleasure from the announcement that I have successfully survived the several sensational ordeals of the German phase of World War II, the late. I'm about the last Prisoner of War to be liberated and shall be flown to a base hospital (for routine check — I'm still in one piece) and thence, by air once more, I hope, to the U.S.. If all goes smoothly I should be on native soil within a week. I've a sixty-day furlough and several hundred bucks awaiting me:— a somewhat cheerful situation by which you may indirectly benefit providing you haven't got married or some damned thing. The happy combination of ready cash and free time will enable me to visit your lovely self—

FORM 539 A

in Washington, I presume. You will, I
hope, find my company at least
entertaining in that I've a great
number of fascinating and fantastic
adventures to relate. At any rate,
dear one, I shall shortly get in
touch with you and give my
respectful attention while you express
oppinions on this and other
matters.

Much love.

Kurt

P.S. I look sort of starved.

FORM 539 A

From:

To: JANE M. COX
96TH & N. COLLEGE AVE.
INDIANAPOLIS, IND.

PFC. KURT VONNEGUT, JR
12102964, U.S. ARMY

(CENSOR'S STAMP)

See Instruction No. 2

(Sender's complete address above)

MAY 29 - 1945

DEAR WOOFY:

SOME ANONYMOUS PERSON HAS STARTED A LOVE LETTER
HERE AND LEFT IT UNFINISHED ON THIS DESK. HAD
I FOLLOWED MY FIRST IMPULSE TO CRUMPLE IT
UP AND THROW IT AWAY, A JEWEL WOULD HAVE
BEEN LOST FOREVER. I SHALL HERE RECORD IT FOR
POSTERITY AND SEEKERS OF BEAUTY—— THE SENTIMENTS
ARE MINE:

"HELLO HONNY

    WELL I GEST YOU THOUGHT I WAS NOT GOING
TO WRITE YOU BUT I HAVE NOT FORGOT YOU I
THINK OF YOU ALL THE TIME"

—— AND THAT'S THE TROOT. I'VE BEEN FLOWN
TO A HUGE P.O.W. REPATRIATION CAMP NEAR
LE HAVRE, FRANCE. SHIPPING IS ALL TIED UP BUT
IF MY LUCK HOLDS OUT I SHOULD BE HOME
IN A MONTH. YOU'LL BE HAPPY TO KNOW
THAT I CAN'T RECEIVE MAIL HERE.

    I'VE A SIXTY-DAY FURLOUGH AWAITING
ME. PERHAPS I SHALL CALL ON YOU.

    AS EVER, YOUR CHUM——

                    KURT

HAVE YOU FILLED IN COMPLETE
ADDRESS AT TOP?

REPLY BY
V···MAIL

HAVE YOU FILLED IN COMPLETE
ADDRESS AT TOP?

22

16—28143-5 ☆ U. S. GOVERNMENT PRINTING OFFICE I 1943

To: KURT VONNEGUT
WILLIAMS CREEK
INDIANAPOLIS, IND.

From:
PFC. KURT VONNEGUT, JR.
12102964 — R.A.M.P
U.S. ARMY, FRANCE

(CENSOR'S STAMP) See Instruction No. 2 (Sender's complete address above)

DEAR FAMILY: JUNE 4, 1945

I'VE BEEN TOLD THAT WE, THE LAST OF THE
LIBERATED AMERICAN P.O.W.'s IN EUROPE, WILL BE
ON BOARD A SHIP WITHIN SEVEN (7) DAYS — OR BY
MONDAY, JUNE 11TH. I SUPPOSE THE TRIP WILL
TAKE ABOUT ANOTHER WEEK SO THAT WOULD SET
MY REPATRIATION DATE NEAR JUNE 18TH. THIS
DATE IS HIGHLY THEORETICAL SO DON'T COUNT ON
IT — BUT I'LL BE HOME PRETTY DAMNED QUICK.
I'LL PHONE OR TELEGRAPH AS SOON AS I HIT
NATIVE SOIL. I'M TO BE SENT TO ATTERBURY
WHERE I EXPECT TO GET MY SIXTY-DAY FURLOUGH
WITHIN THIRTY-SIX (36) HOURS.

THIS IS MY LAST COMMUNIQUE FROM
THE EUROPEAN THEATER OF OPERATIONS. HOPE
ALL ARE WELL —— I HOPE THAT LIKE HELL.

MUCH LOVE.

KURT-JR.

REPLY BY
V···-MAIL
16—28142-0 ☆ U. S. GOVERNMENT PRINTING OFFICE / 1943

If Thou survive my well-contented day
When that churl Death my bones with dust shall cover,
And shalt by fortune once more re-survey
These poor rude lines of thy deceased lover;
Compare them with the bettering of the time,
And though they be outstripp'd by every pen,
Reserve them for my love, not for their rhyme
Exceeded by the height of happier men.
O then vouchsafe me but this loving thought--
'Had my friend's muse grown with this growing age,
A dearer birth than this his love had brought,
To march in ranks of better equipage:
     But since he died, and poets better prove,
     Theirs for their style I'll read, his for his love.'

               *   *   *   *

     To follow this wonderfully pertinant wisdom with words of my own makes me, I know, one of the most insoucient fools alive today.   To do what I have just done is the equivalent of starting off a concert with the 1812 Overture.   Anything I say now, from an eye-witness account of the Crucifixion of Christ to a discussion of price-fluctuations at the Kansas City Hog Market today, will be redundant.   I've bloody-goddamn-well had it.   The sonofabitch who wrote that Sonnet has bloody-goddamn-well said everything.

     However, Darling, this love affair of ours is a thing apart, an entirely specific situation which concerns, and could only concern, though time be infinite, us.   And I think, Angel, that it is a sorry commentary on our avowed individuality if we can throw Shakespeare about us and have him fit like a suit from Brookes Brothers.   (((One hour has expired, Sweety, since I mis-spelled Brooks.   You are going to be married to a damned fool, Darling.   Do you know what he did during that hour?   He tried to write a

Sonnet.   The kid's got courage, you've got to admit.   He
thought he could knock one out every bit as good as
"Thy bosom is endeared with all hearts..." and he thought
that it would make you very happy to think that he
was easily as good as Shakespeare.   Well, he knows now,
though not without a trace of bitterness.   Johnny Mercer
wrote the words to "Goody, goody" in 15 minutes.   I
think I could too, though I'd hate myself in the morning.
I draw inspiration from the wrong people.   I'll write
us a Sonnet if it takes me the rest of my life; but I've
bloody-goddamn-well had it tonight.   Stephen Foster had
a dirty piece of paper in his pocket when they found his
body.   On it was written: "Sweet friends and gentle
hearts...")))

     I love you, Darling.   When one person from the
Corn Belt misses another person from the Corn Belt he
doesn't say, for a very good reason: "Shall I compare
thee to a summer's day?"   Hell no, he doesn't.   He
says "Holy Jesus Christ, Angel; I miss you like hell.
Dammit, Sweety, I'm going nuts without you.   I ache
all over.   I'll blow my top."   And I will, too.

     Anticlimax Department: my brother, one strange
Bernard Vonnegut, will be here on this coming week-end
if all goes well.   He wishes me to go with him to
Cambridge.   This will I do.   It is my intention to
live there in pseudo-bachelorhood for a period of a
few days, during which I will pick up any brutally
frank marital hints which he may care to throw my way.
My bosom, endeared with these lewd jewels, will I then
take to Washington and thereupon unload same in your
loving arms.   Love, love, love; love, dammit, love.

1945:

BACK HOME

ON JULY 2, 1945, ON THE WAY FROM FRANCE BACK TO CAMP
Atterbury, Indiana, Kurt stopped in Washington, D.C., to see Jane and
convince her to break it off with her other suitors. They continued on
to Indianapolis together, as Jane wanted to see her mother, who had had
another nervous breakdown. Kurt proposed marriage in Indianapolis,
and Jane accepted.

Although he had talked about marriage no fewer than twenty-four
times in his letters, this was Kurt's second real proposal. The first time
he proposed in person had been one month after the death of his
mother. It was an unusual proposal. He'd been to the dentist and was
wearing his extracted molar around his neck. He ripped his shirt open,
revealing the bloody tooth, proclaimed how much he loved her, and
asked for her hand. My mother always told this story in a kind of
baffled way. I don't think she liked that approach.

The second proposal was more traditional, and she accepted,
returning to Washington wearing an engagement ring made from half
the stones on his mother's wedding ring. We don't know exactly what
finally tipped the balance in Kurt's favor. Perhaps he was the loudest,

most persistent voice in the room. Perhaps she fell in love with the writing and the dreams they were creating together . . .

ON AUGUST 6 AND 9, 1945, the United States dropped atomic bombs on Hiroshima and Nagasaki, killing more than 200,000 people.

One month later, on September 1, 1945, Kurt and Jane married in a Quaker ceremony on the backyard terrace of Jane's house in Indianapolis. Allie was the maid of honor. The young couple honeymooned at French Lick Resort on the edge of the Hoosier National Forest. Family legend has it that Jane made Kurt read *The Brothers Karamazov* on their honeymoon. He admired her excellent education and deferred to her often regarding literature.

At the end of the month, Kurt had to report to Fort Riley, Kansas, to finish his military duty. He was assigned to the secretarial pool. It is here, at Jane's coaxing, that he began to write short stories. Jane had always thought she'd be a writer too, but she quickly recognized her husband's tremendous talent (even before he did) and put her own dreams and ambitions aside in order to help him. Jane lived at home in Indianapolis during this period, seeing old friends and spending time with her father. She briefly had a job selling dresses in a department store, but most of her time was spent editing Kurt's first stories and submitting them to agents.

It was during this time that Kurt, after working on several short stories, realized he needed to write about his experience in the war.

Kurt Vonnegut, Jr.
Ridge Road, Williams Creek
Indianapolis, Indiana

AIR MAIL

Miss   Jane   Marie   Cox
3752   W   Street   N.W.
Washington,   D.C.

Tell me where is Fancy bred,
Or in the heart, or in the head;
How begot, how nourished:
            Reply, reply.

DARLING ~ ♡

ENCLOSED YOU WILL FIND A HIGHLY SYMBOLIC EXPRESSION OF HOW I HAVE FELT ALL DAY. I'M GOING TO SEE YOUR MOTHER TOMORROW — TO HELP HER GET THE BLUE-PRINT FOR OUR WEDDING FINISHED, BECAUSE, SWEETY, METHINKS SHE'LL HAVE OCCASION TO USE IT BEFORE SEPTEMBER 14TH. WHAT DO YOU THINK?

FEARLESS FERN OF BELCHER FARMS STARTED POPULATING THE WORLD WITH LESSER SALUKIS AT 9:30 TONIGHT AND HAS, AT THIS WRITING, PRODUCED EIGHT. SHE IS A WONDERFUL MOTHER. HOW THE WORD "BITCH" FELL INTO DIS-REPUTE I DON'T KNOW. IF THESE ARE THE ENDS OF PROMIS-CUITY, THEN PROMISCUITY IS AN UNSELFISH AND BEAUTIFUL THING. AFTER SEEING THE PUPS I'VE DECIDED TO NEVER HAVE ANYTHING BUT A LESSER SALUKI. EACH ONE IS THE SWEETEST LITTLE SON OF A BITCH THAT YOU EVER SAW. I AM TOUCHED.

I LOVE YOU, DARLING. OF ALL THE MANY TIMES WE'VE PARTED, THIS IS THE FIRST TIME YOU'VE TAKEN A BIG BLOODY CHUNK OF ME WITH YOU. THERE IS NO SENSE

IN OUR BEING APART. LET US WED
SOON. IF BERNARD COMES THIS WEEK-END
I'LL BE WITH YOU IN WASHINGTON BY
AUGUST 15TH, AT LEAST.

At THE BASE OF THE PEDESTAL
UPON WHICH RESTS THE ANIMAL
IN ME, YOU WILL SEE A SMALL DOGHOUSE.
IF YOU WILL RECALL, THE ANIMAL IN
ME ONCE FITTED VERY NICELY INSIDE
OF IT.

I forgot to tell you that we now have a checking
account at the Fletcher Trust Company. I opened it day
before yesterday with all the money I earned working for
Adolph Hitler. Mr. Dodd took care of me. He gave me
25 blank checks and a little mottled red and black book
which is supposed to tell us how much money we have. I
have already lost the little mottled red and black book
so I will have to tell you how much we have from memory.
I think it is $458.98. I am very proud and happy because
it represents what Mrs. Wainwright waited for before she
got married--$security.

I L*O*V*E Y*O*U

Outside of our prospective wedding and the estab-
lishment of a new World's record for sustained bliss, we
have these irons on the fire: one medium length article to
the New Yorker, five very short humorous articles to the
Post; and one murder mystery and one very tedius story of
my adventures in Germany, both embryonic. All of which
gives me the dazzling idea of covering the lampshade of
our Champagn bottle lamp with rejection slips.

A*N*D A*M P*E*R*P*E*T*U*A*L*L*Y, P*A*I*N*F*U*L*L*Y

I can't tell you anything more about my trip to
Washington. But, dammit, Darling, Bernard should be here
soon--withing two or three days. And ten days should see
us, you and me, the insoluable, undeniable, admirable and
God-given unit, electron and proton, together and panting.
I will thereupon give wistful Washington bureaucracy a
brief glance at the amorous genius that has so captivated
your lovely self, say a few modest words about the whopping
big sparkler, and take you away from it all.

C*O*N*S*C*I*O*U*S O*F R*E*C*E*I*V*I*N*G M*B*R*E*

Bernard has sent us some pictures of Peter--his
son. Peter looks astonishingly much like his father
which isn't astonishing after all except that it's hard to
belieye that there are now two of them on Earth.

T*H*A*N I C*A*N E*V*E*R H*O*P*E T*O G*I*V*E.

A b s t r a c t i o n:Two happy termites, baring their teeth
                     as they prepare to gnaw down a 5000
                     year-old Redwood.

F*E*E*L T*H*E S*A*M*E W*A*Y A*N*D W*E C*A*N*T M*I*S*S*********

L o v e . . . .   Kurt

---

xxxxxx 7

Cripes but I'm d r o w z y, Cutie:

Poor Woofy, working her fingers to the bone 40 hours a week
in sweltering Washington while her no good fiance sleeps
till noon, drinks beer all day and goes barefoot.   Not only
that, but he got a Goddamn rejection slip from the snotty
Saturday Evening Post today, that's what.   He cancelled
his subscription in a hurry, believe me.   Bastards.

This is the time of the month that you're supposed to be in
rough shape, isn't it?   Oh gosh, Sweety, I'm sorry.   I
wish I'd designed women.   God may be a pretty sweet old
cuss, but he's no engineer. I wouldn't alter your chassis
lines a mite, not yours, but I would put a new set of works
inside.   There's no damn sense in producing a perfidious
gadget that goes flooey every 30 days.   Dames has got it
rough kiddo and youse has got my sympathy.   Also, I love
you love you love you, and when we are wed I shall speak
softly and stroke your forehead and keep you perpetually
pregnant so you will be in trouble just once every nine
months.   But yi, Honey, what trouble.   Ouch.   Dames has
soiny got it rough, kiddo.   XXXXXX   Give me a big
yummy wet kiss.   mmmmMmmmMMMmmmmmmMMMMMMMMMmmmmMMMMMMMM

Sweety, promise me something.   You scare me when you say
that I would have been Shakespeare had I lived then. And
you scare me when you say that I am going to create the
literature of 1945 onwards and upwards.   Angel, will you
stick by me if it goes backwards and downwards?   Holy
smokes, Angel: what if I turn out to be just plain folks?
Oh my God--I want to kiss you kiss you kiss you.   Rrrrrr

I wrotechez a letter yesterday but forgot to mail it so
you'll get two today.   How was it to go without one for
a day?

Tell Peter that I'll get her an orchid after I've tasted the
pork chops.   Tell Issy that I love her dearly (which is
the truth), that I shall bring her an orchid, with a garden-
ia for interest, and that after I sell the stupendous novel
that you keep saying I am going to write? I will send her
an orchid a week for the rest of her life.

For goodness sakes, Woofy, do I have to do **all** the thinking
for us?   Call Miss Phillipps immediately before she gives
it all away!   I must say you're pretty thick about financial matters.   You'd better send me your pay check before
that goes out the window too.

Here's a narsty problem.   Visualize if you can our return
from our h o n e y m o o n.   Either we stay at our house
suxxax or at your house.   I'm personally plumping for our
house, because I'm damned if I've got the courage to take
your mother's and father's daughter to bed in front of them.
I'll dash out the front door and turn up 20 years later in
Hong Kong with amnesia.   No, dear, I will take you to bed
here.   That way, both of us will feel very married.   At
your house we would feel too married.   Agreed?

                    LOVE   K

77777777777777777777777777777777777777777777777777777777777

Holy Jesus, darling, darling, darling:

I will have to get on the ball in a hurry if this letter
is to be mailed to you this morning.   I try to knock out one
a day, because I want to, for one reason; and because you might
think that I don't love you any more--which would make you
one of the most greeviously misinformed persons alive.   Sweety,
I usually (Listen to the guy: he's written two letters so far
and he says usually) write to you in the evenings.   But last
night I have had an extremely hot streak and am very pleased
with the results before me now. Four short articles,
Angel, that I hope will land me a contract with the Post. This
is the current pipe dream, Lovey, and I want you to share it.
Perhaps you have noticed the section of the Post called
Postscripts.   It is supposed to be funny, but it isn't. A
lot of people contribute to it every week and are doubtless
under contract at about $40 a whack, I should say.   That,
Sweety, is no mean gravy for what they produce, and I plan
to get some of it for us.   Mainly because I am funnier than
anyone they've got now. That's how good I am.

Fern's litter stopped at eight. She delivered them all
herself, with nox apparent effort. Allie and I observed
that it is a great deal easier to have young in little chunks
instead of one whopping big one.   There are four males and
four females.   I think that we can find homes for them all.
As the only Lesser Salukis in the World, they are becoming
quite famous all over Indianapolis.   However, in looking over
prospective foster-parents, I made a discovery which is painful.
It is a violent contradiction of Vonnegut's Axiom: People who
don't like dogs aren't much good.   Phoebe hates dogs! She
says that they lick her leg-makeup off.   We've thought up one
name so far--"G. Rover Cleveland". Do you think that is
funny?   Sometimes I do, sometimes I don't; but I love you
and miss you all of the time.

Mrs. Wainwright called yesterday.   She said this: "I've
just got it through my head that you two kids are really going
to get married on September 14th. Forgonnessake, what would
you like for a wedding present?"   I was very sweet to her,
Woofy, Parlor Pink that I am, and I thanked her for such
generous thoughts, but I couldn't give her much of an answer.
Not without your being here (a condition which will be effected
shortly).   She made the suggestion of luggage.   I recall
your having said something about needing luggage so I told
her that perhaps that is what we needed.   Well, Angel,
she said that if you wanted to pick out some pieces in Washington, she would love to have you send her the description of
them, the store and the salesman's name.   That is, if you
want luggage.   I suppose stuff like this will be cropping
up all of the time. We ought to pick out silver and china
patterns plenty quick or we won't get any.

Alex called to tell me that our pictures will be ready
on Saturday.   I'll send them or bring them to Washington
with me. Dammit, Darling, Bernard should be here in a few
more days.   I want to see him very much, as he is, after
all, my blood brother.   But I don't think I'll go to Cambridge
with him.   After he leaves I will try to catch a Washington-
bound bomber from Stout Field.

Golly but that was a sweet letter I got this morning. And
a post-card, too. When I say something it sounds like a little
boy beating on a rain barrel.   When you say something it sounds
like kettledrums. "Then we will live outside of time and space,
and ignore it."

                    *   *   *   *

A B s t r a c t i o n : two warm pink presences in a cool blue
                        cloud, ten thousand feet above Earth.

                  *   *   *   *   *

LOVE (1)   We've got a wonderful lot of fun ahead of
                     us, Darling. You needn't have instructed
    LOVE (2)   me to smile at you as you come down the
                     aisle.   This, being a love match, re-
        LOVE(3)   quires no outside coaching in such
                         matters.   Of course I'll smile.
            LOVE (4)   Naturally, and with all the joy in
                          my fantastically lucky soul.
        LOVE (5)

        LOVE (6)

        LOVE (7)

    This is a picture of a Sodium Chloride (NaCl--table salt)
molecule.   It is particularly interesting because the molecule
is as large as any specific lump of salt.   It goes infin-
itely on, but always in these proportions: one atom sodium, one
atom chlorine.   It is a very
stable substance.   - Cl - Na - Cl -

                        - Na - Cl - Na -

                        - Cl - Na - Cl -

    I Hope that   - WOOFY - KURT - WOOFY -   we can go on
and on chrystal-   vizing, growing
bigger and bigger: - KURT - WOOFY - KURT -   one atom of Kurt
to one atom of   Woofy.

                         - WOOFY - KURT - WOOFY -

    I think maybe I've been a bore in this letter.   But
dammit, Darling--I love you so much that I always try too
hard.

                    L o v e ,   L o v e l y

                            KURT -

August 7th, 1945

Woofy, Darling:

Your moody husband is ecstatically happy just now. He
has an idea and is excited. He is feverish, leering and
chain smoking. Gordon Thompson called not five minutes
ago, to congratulate us and to ask if I was interested in
teaching at Orchard. Oh golly, Sweety, quel bon idea!
I would love it, wouldn't you?

Unstable as I am, I think it would be preposterous for
me to think of writing for a living. I'll write, yes, and
so will you, Darling, but we ought only to write what we feel
should be written. In making a living for us and the
seven children, I want to be one of Frank Lloyd Wright's
(When Democracy Builds) hewers of wood and drawers of water.
I want to work as a newspaper man or a teacher. Being honest
about myself, I realize that I have not the genius to dedicate
my life to creating phantasmagoria. We both have naiive
and entirely charming intellects, Angel, and we represent
lovable tendencies in the divine direction of the dignity of
man. We are good, but we are not great. This above all,
to thine own self be true... We have spasms of spectacular
inspiration, Cuddles, but there is no sustained, driving
urge to realize a cleanly cut idea. We are in the blithe
pursuit of happiness, with the happy abandon of a child in
the Five and Ten. Our marriage will be such a complete
consumation of what we both want that we shall want for very
little else. Maladjustment and dissatisfaction drive people
on dizzy quests that characterize great men and women of art.
I am glad that I have found the Holy Grail in you. Expression
in flesh and blood, yours and mine. Two fused in love, heat
and sweat--sight, sound, smell, feel and taste.

****

Bernard has just called from Dayton. He will be here
at 4:40 today. He'll stay until Sunday. I'm leaving on Sunday
via any means Ican muster. I'm going to try to catch a
bomber from Stout Field.

I wrote to the Miami Beach Redistribution Center and they
sent me a booklet all about it. I will send it on to you.
Beyond a doubt it will be heaven, Darling.

A b s t r a c t i o n: Slope

Foal Soul Soul Shoal: Fully Foul Shoal. Fool Foal Soul, Fool
Shoal. Shall Souls Surely Slope? Shall Foul Foal Souls Slope?
Shall Shoals? Nope.

I am a s q u i r r e l. #$%&½@¾--poor neglected things never
get used. ₫₫n'# you $ee #ha# I love you more #h₫n ½,¼
& ¾? D₫ you love me #%?

KURT XXXXXXX

149

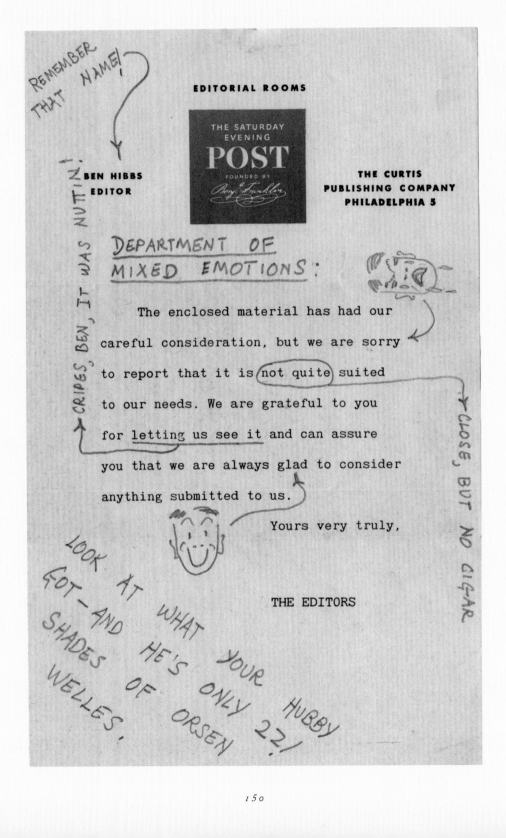

EDITORIAL ROOMS

THE SATURDAY EVENING
POST
FOUNDED BY
Benj. Franklin

BEN HIBBS
EDITOR

THE CURTIS
PUBLISHING COMPANY
PHILADELPHIA 5

REMEMBER THAT NAME!

CRIPES, BEN, IT WAS NUTTIN'!

DEPARTMENT OF
MIXED EMOTIONS:

        The enclosed material has had our

careful consideration, but we are sorry

to report that it is (not quite) suited

to our needs. We are grateful to you

for letting us see it and can assure

you that we are always glad to consider

anything submitted to us.

                        Yours very truly,

                        THE EDITORS

CLOSE, BUT NO CIGAR

LOOK AT WHAT YOUR HUBBY GOT — AND HE'S ONLY 22! SHADES OF ORSEN WELLES.

DEAR WOOFY-DARLING:

OCEAN: THROUGH THE UNDULATING SURF AND TIDES OF TWO BILLION PEOPLE I AM HERE AND YOU ARE THERE: HUSBAND AND WIFE PARTED IN VIOLATION OF MORALS AND NATURE, AND IN BRUTAL OPPOSITION TO OUR OWN INNOCENT, HONEST AND JUST WILLS. IS THERE A SOLITARY VILLAIN TO BE SINGLED OUT AND BLAMED?

WHAT'S TO BE DONE, ANGEL? SOMETHING, SURELY. WE MUST WAIT FOR MY DISCHARGE — DECEMBER, JANUARY, FEBRUARY? BUT NEED WE BE APART? I'VE PRAYED TO GOD THAT WHAT HE HATH THEREFORE JOINED TOGETHER, LET NOT MAN PUT ASUNDER. I AM ALSO

REFERRING MY BLEEDING HEART
TO UNCLE LOUIS LUDLOW. WE
SHALL SEE JUST WHAT THE
OCEAN MAY BE ABLE TO YIELD
TO THE SHORE.

MY ADDRESS IS —

HQ. CO.
AGF RD #3
FORT RILEY, KANSAS
AND A DISMAL SPOT IT IS,
A VOID. YOU'D BE BORED
AND DESOLATE WERE YOU TO
LIVE IN NEARBY JUNCTION
CITY OR MANHATTAN —— SO
THAT'S OUT! MY GOD, WHAT
A WASTE OF TIME!

DESOLATION TO MELANCHOLY
TO APATHY TO BLISS TO ECSTASY
TO BLISS TO APATHY TO MELANCHOLY
TO DESOLATION TO MELANCHOLY
TO APATHY TO... LIKE A
PENDULUM MY MIND HAS BEEN

SWINGING SINCE I KISSED YOU LAST, SLEEPY AND TEARFUL. I CARRIED SOME OF YOUR TEARS AWAY WITH ME, ON MY LASHES, CHEEKS AND MOUTH. BLESSED ARE THE MEEK, FOR THEY SHALL INHERIT THE EARTH. BLESSED ARE JANE AND KURT, FOR THEIRS WAS THE KINGDOM OF HEAVEN. UNQUALIFIED HEAVEN IT WAS AND SOON SHALL BE, DARLING.

I'VE WRITTEN A GREAT DEAL OF GARBAGE TODAY AND YESTERDAY, TRYING TO GIVE EXPRESSION TO THE EMOTIONS THAT HAVE KEPT ME SLEEPLESS

AT NIGHT AND CHAIN-SMOKING
THROUGH WET GRAY DAYS. I
CAN'T DO IT BECAUSE I'M
OVERWHELMED AND SUFFOCATED
AND AWESTRICKEN BY THE
MIGHT AND SPLENDOR AND
SWEETNESS AND FURY OF
THE FLOOD OF LOVE AND
WONDER THAT YOU HAVE
CAUSED TO BURST FROM
ME. I LOVE YOU TERRIBLY.

IT REALLY DID HAPPEN — EVERY
SUBLIME SECOND OF IT!

Oct. 3, 1945

Dear Heart;

I think that I'll get a
letter from you today—Wednesday,
and so, rather than drool on...
I've nothing worth saying other
than that there is a demon
in the pit of my stomach, with
hands and feet of ice. His
only pleasure seems to be to
stroke the walls and ceiling
of my stomach with his icy
hands and shuffle his frozen
feet on its floor. Golly, Angel,
it's almost grotesque. I love
you and miss you so much.
Darling, Darling, Darling,
    I've yet to be assigned.
Louis Ludlow should have
got my letter by now. Wait.
Wait. Wait.

Tell me, dear one, are you perchance with child, half mine? If so, I see no reason for anything but rapture on our parts. We can (because of what mom left to me) afford it — and if it has been conceived in this last month, no child was ever conceived in more love or in a more blesséd union.

Every Angel, even if Louis Ludlow can't or won't get me shipped to Harrison or Atterbury, I shall be home, almost certainly by Christmas.

I'm reading Dragon Harvest. I quote from page

26. "The provoking fellow came strolling in, bland and i̲n̲s̲o̲v̲c̲i̲a̲n̲t̲ . . ."

Oh, Darling, I feel like hell, having made your life for the present the dull thing it must be. Please, dear Heart, go on loving me. I'll be home, soon. It can't go on much longer. And then, Sweety, we'll go to Chicago as we first planned it. And you shall change from Alyosha to Zossima and I shall change from Kolya to Alyosha.

Much love — Cutie

Kurt —

DEAR WIFE:

This letter is the death
rattle of three cancerous
years: three festering
Witches whose abscesses
dripped butchery and best-
iality into a seething broth
concoted of greed, apathy and ignorance. They
are dead, thank God, and we'll bury these unholy sisters so we'll not be upset by the ran-
cid stench of their putrifying.   They are
dead.   For them this is

-THE END-

We are very alive, Darling, and young and
full of warm love--with a lovely lust for
each other and for wisdom.   For us this
is

-CHAPTER I-

I love you now, Sweetheart, and I'll love you
always.   You are a beautiful wife.   I was
made to love and to make love to only you. To
do otherwise, Woofy, is physically impossible
for me.
The smug and blessed cat above is a graphic
description of how your husband felt on the
eve of his being freed to spend every remaining
minute of his life with you.   You should be
proud to be loved so terribly much.   Oh golly,
Darling...

XXXXXXX

KURT

Saturday night
October 6, 1945

Dear Woofy, wifey:

Somehow — time passes.
I've just come from
taking a shower; it's
9:30 P.M. and I'm about
to go to bed. But first
I want to tell you about
what I thought in the
shower.

It started with an
idea of yours. Remember
when you were standing
barefoot in the gentle
little surf on the Roney
Plaza Beach (formerly
the property of God)? You
had your dress up to your

159

heavenly hips and an almost full moon glowed big, stupid and beautiful above us. You were wondering what distant beaches certain of the molecules in the surf lapping at your feet had visited.

I was thinking about that in the shower and wondering at the tinyness of molecules. And then I thought: "Why, some of Woofy's molecules must be with me now—in my pores or lungs or mouth or even my blood. For we have been as wonderfully close to each other as any two people can get without becoming <u>actually and forever</u> the same person—so in that love making some of your molecules surely found new homes in me." And I came upstairs, smiling cheerfully and humming Humoresque and thinking that this had altogether been the nicest, loveliest and most wonderful thought I have had since we parted.

And then, sweet Angel, another thought came to me—: an _obvious_ thought that made my first idea look like what a spring thunderstorm makes the popping of a Champagne cork look like.

Think of that part of me that is now inside of you.

—— Darling, I love you so! What heavenly love we should be making at this dull and brutal moment!

ppppp Good night, Angel. WURST

Poor Sweet Darling...Bored? Lonesome? Oh damn.
_____

       At least you shan't want for love and letters. Those two things I can give you in quantity. That much nourishment I can give you.

       I've yet to hear from Louis. Have you? At any rate I shall be home, with a discharge, within eighty days...so start checking them off. Everything points to it. We will surely be able to enter the Winter Quarter (when does it start,Sweety?) at Chicago. Know full well that with a full little tummy on myself, my wife and my children, my motive in life will be to work and study and do what is in my power to give something that is damned good for the whole World. Generally, Peace and Democracy. However, full tummies come first. First things come first. The main motive is you,as I am more animal than spiritual. I will do anything to keep you loving me. What by-products that come from that love the world is welcome to. You, alone, are justification for my living. A pox on the rest of creation--but you give me some gorgeous ideas that would probably make the rest of creation, if it insists on being on Earth with us, happier.

       This is a stinking big piece of paper. My love-maker is a great deal more articulate, expressive and poetic than this typewriter. Love was conceived so great, so powerful, that it is beyond our comprehension to describe accurately in words. Its absolute description is in a blissful series of sensations. That physical description of how much we love each other IS absolute and adequate. And I almost weep for not being able to make you feel, to make you know certainly and ecstatically how much I love you. And want, for at least a second or two, to be you. I don't think that very many people honestly feel that way. If I am superhuman in any respect, it is in that respect--I love you most awfully, Woofy.

       I shall have a three day pass soon. It is impossible for me to come to Indianapolis for it--but could we meet in Kansas City? It is a very slick town full of bars and nightclubs...........................and beds, Angel. When should I ask for the pass? Or can you make it? Do you think it would be worth while?

S   O   O   N   !

Dearly beloved:

There was a big racoon on the library steps last
night. He was quite friendly and I spent most of the evening
fooling around with him. Someone here, I haven't as yet found
out who, brought him up from a coonlet. I've been investigating
the coon business and having them for pets is evidently a pretty
common thing. They will make marvelous pets if they are taken
before their eyes are open, one informant tells me. So, sweety,
we will one day get ourselves a coonlet, before its eyes are
open. Colly, what a nifty pet they are! Tell Allie about
this--and watch her eyes light up.

I'm afraid my story about the rose is terrible, but
after all it's only about the fourth short story I've written
in my life. For my fourth short story I should say that it
is not nearly as repulsive as could be expected. I'll send
the damned thing to you and you send it wherever you like. Just
for variety in rejection slips, send it to the Atlantic first
and then to Esquire. Any changes you see fit to make please
make. This is not a work of art but a grasping at money. I
love money.

I work from 8 to 5 every day. I'm on a 40 hour week
and so take two days off each week. Those two days vary with
the whims of my boss. The bastards (the Army promised that
they wouldn't) have counted my 76 days at home on recuperation
as a furlough so I'll have to scrap like hell to get a furlough.
Theoretically, I haven't had a proper furlough in over a year and
a quarter. That, and this is also theoretical, entitles me to
something over 20 days at home. But I don't think I'll get it.
Oh, Hell, Sweety, Believe me when I say I shall definitely be
home for Christmas--and probably a lot sooner than that. That,
Dear Heart, is not a bad deal for the Army. Time passes somehow.
If you can think of any slick ways (ask Phoebe) that we can lay
away some money during the interum, please write me about them.
I'm simply nuts about money.

It's morning, now.   I've just had my two days off...
Monday and Tuesday.   In that time I've discovered a big river
and a pet racoon so I'm not nearly as lonesome as I was.   I
swear to God that I don't feel like talking to a soul. I haven't
made a single damned friend.   I fugure I've got enough of the
damned things.   The food is terrible and believe me when I
say my mouth waters for some of your cooking.   The food here is
that terrible.   I weep for lack of your cooking. Darling, you
are not the worst cook in the World.

This office is no place for a love letter.   I write my
best love letters in pencil, I think...when I'm full of coffee.
In the morning.   I'll try to abort one from my soul tonight.
When you get a dull affair like this one, I suggest that you refer
back to more inspired works.

I love you most awfully, Darling.

Love...

K̶u̶t̶

ANGEL:

30 days ago we were
married ~ ♡

I am humble and full of
childish gratitude and wonder for
the cool, the sweet, the gentle
and deep, the brilliant, exquisitely
melodic, rhapsodic, rolling, rumbling
thundering, hell-fire burning,
throbbing, bursting, trembling,
sighing, crying, dying, smiling,
sleeping love you gave to me.

The young and warmly
loving two of us in bed are
closer to God than the topmost
spires of the greatest and
most blessed cathedral in
creation. There are three
gates to paradise: through your

eyes, through your lips and
between your thighs. You,
darling, have blessed me and
let me through each of
them — and have, in doing
so, given me immortality
and joy everlasting by
stretching earthly seconds
into ages a billion times
greater than the age of
Sun. What I have said
is blissful truth.
———————— ♡ Small wonder,
darling, that I am humble
and full of childish gratitude.
———————— ♡ Lo, how the mighty
have fallen! Paradise lost.
———————— ♡ Paradise regained?
Please, Please, Please, When?
I ADORE YOU, DARLING

xxxx ⊨⊨⊨ mmm KURT.

Angel:

      I've got the life of Beethoven, War and Peace, and
Brigg's Simplified Calculus going simultaniously. I wish I
had less enthusiasm and more brains. Then again, I find comfort in what seems to me to be an absolute law: PEOPLE ARE
ABSOLUTELY INNOCENT OF WHAT THEY SEEM TO BE. Do you believe
that? There are so many external forces (and the laws of
physics are enough to discourage a man from being what he wants
to be) that I can't see how it would be otherwise. At the
age of 23 I cannot roller-skate and probably never shall learn.
That is absolute--I cannot roller-skate. And yet, had the
proper inclination in the form of chemicals, or had the proper
person insisted that I learn to roller-skate, I would probably
be quite good at it by now. But they didn't. So at 23 I
cannot roller-skate. And I maintain that I am blameless of
my ignorance of the sport. You, Dear Heart, will never ever
be able to carry a tune without changing key every three bars.
You will never be able to do it. My sister can carry a tune,
and has such a good ear for it that she can sing two-part harmony.
You are blameless for not being George Gershwin. George Gershwin
is blameless for not being you. There can be no argument as
to who is BETTER--you, me, George Gershwin, John Dillinger,
George Washington Carver, Arthur Rodebaugh. If there weren't
a God, He would have to be invented. The present synthesis does
not gibe with the human facts. Here is a chance for real genius.
The greatest man to ever live will be the one that invents the
real God, and presents the World with a book of His teachings.
A Bible written in a Lunatic Asylum may be the answer. If the
physical scientists are the men destined to stumble onto the
answer, then it will be quiet investigators like my brother, who,
driven up obscure passage-ways of research by their curiosity,
and not by General Motors, DuPont and the War Department. Speed,
destructive power, efficiency, volume, load capacity--the answer
wont be found among these. Perhaps I've told you how I hate
all the bright-eyed young men I've met in the Army: engineering
students, chemists: handsome, tall, intelligent, clean. I think
I hate them because they think the answer to a better World
(and the means to a bigger income) is in their taking the groundwork
layed by Descartes, Newton, Pascal, Aristotle etc. and turning it
into speed, destructive power, efficiency, volume, load capacity.
That is why I love my brother as much as I do. He does not think
that way. Of the three of us--Bernard, Allie, and Myself--Bernard
has the best, at least the most far-reaching, chance of doing
the World a great favor. Allie will turn out marvelous children,
I'm not at all certain what I'll do (because I am ignorant), but
Bernard KNOWS an awful lot of important things, and is SKILLFUL
in applying them.

      What a screwy letter, Darling. I had no idea that it
would turn out this way. Maybe with a little serious application
we will get to be as admirable as Bernard. It's worth a lifetime
of trying.

   n   Love.....xxxxxxx

Kurt

Dear Woofy, wifey:

Since we're both so nuts about money, why
don't we think about cracking Hollywood? As writers, or you might do right
well in dress-design...but it's a possibility.   I see every damned movie
they bring to this place, and if we couldn't direct better ones I'll eat a
tube of ortho-gynol.   Last night's movie was the pay-off:Betty Grable in
the "Dolly Sisters." Miss it if you possibly can.   Legs, legs, legs,
and not one pair of them half as good as yours.   You spoiled the movies
for me, Baby.   The Johnsons are going to write Leo Burnett about me.
A little later maybe Mr. Burnett will write somebody else about me.   And
then maybe that somebody will write someone else and we'll have jobs in
Hollywood.   We might be able to do a lot of good there if we got into an
influential spot.   I have lovely day dreams.   My big problem now is to
live long enough to realize some of them. Rich man, poor man, begger man,
thief; Doctor, Lawyer, Merchant, Chief.

You, dear heart, pay Mr. Janus. And
while you're dabbling in high finance, go down to Walks and have it assessed.
Then, Angel, tell Mr. Janus what the sparkler is worth and take out another
policy.   I'll deposit about $150 I've got coming to me around the first of
November.   Your first (and let us hope next to last) allotment check
should roll in about that time.   Don't fret if it doesn't come right
away. I'm not at all certain when it is supposed to come.

This office, Message Center, has been
busy as hell recently.   I'll never be able to do office work—not that I
ever considered it.   All I do is sit and type, recording correspondence
coming in and out of AGFRD#3.   It's driving me nuts.   The job carries a
sergeant's rating but this place is too slovenly to give it to me.   Also,
I am becoming something of a head-ache to the more industrious members of
the staff.   I brood.   Did you know that the Navy and Marines have discharged
all of their ex-PW's with more than 60 days in prison.   I'm nuts about the
Army and hope all our sons go to Military School.

I love you very much, Darling.   Leave it
at that until I am able to CONVINCE you how much I do love you.

Kurt-

169

                              Saturday morning...20 Oct 45
                              Time passes, somehow........

Woofy, Darling...

        I'M back at work again.   I tried to sleep on the
train last night but couldn't because of a new malady that
will eventually drive me completely nuts: plotosis.   More
and more short-story plots flash through my mind. I was in
a frenzy because I was certain that I would forget them all
(it was just like having someone tell me story after story)
--and I didn't have a pencil.   So I took my Good Conduct,
Purple Heart and ETO Ribbon farce in technichler and used the
pin on the back of it to stencil out notes. I've got about
twenty stories to write now.   It would certainly contribute
to their fire and vitality if we could get some indication
that they are worth MONEY.   One story, which I will
write tonight, will be written with the smug and snotty
purpose of being a thing which cannot be published during
my unappreciated life-time.

        George has written to tell me that he is discharged,
and that Skip will also be out soon.   Judging from a story
which some insoucient G.I. has tacked on the barracks bulletin
board, demobilization, especially in the Ground Forces (Playground for Brasshatdom) has been a sorry piece of blunder and
low comedy.   Congress has been asking the Army to furlough
men until their time for discharge comes up or to mass-discharge
all men with over two years service.   These plans have
disappeared into the Pentagon.   Whenever Congress asks what
has become of them they are told that the plans are "under
study."   Ha!   Well, according to the article, all hell is
bound to cut loose this coming Monday morning on the floor of
Congress--and the civilians who run this country are damned
well going to get some action. Leave us pray.

        Of course I love you, darling.   But I don't want
to talk about love--not here and now. A brief survey of this
office indicates that I am the only person in the place that
knows anything about it. How could I help but love you and
marry you when you taught me everything I know about it--and
how it's made.

        Tonight I will write you a story.   It wont be a
pretty story.   Someday I will write a pretty love story about
us--but not tonight.

                        Love...

                              Kurt

                              170

LAMBIKINS:

        I have requested that the sons of bitches kindly leave me alone long enough to write a letter to you. One letter that came through here today began: "Dear War Department." It was from Kentucky, naturally. Another one, forewarded to us from the White House, requesting a discharge, began, "Dear President," and ended, after four blotchy, smeared, unpunctuated pages with, "Thank you for taking a little time to consider my case (It took me ten minutes--I wonder how long it took Harry). I know that you probably have a lot more important things to do than to have to listen to a plain G.I.'s troubles (He probably got that warped idea from reading newspapers) but I know that you are the only person that can help me in my trouble." His main trouble, the one that Harry must at this moment be bending every sinew and brain-cell to rectify, was that he had been in the Army since May 26th (The day I was returned to American hands) and didn't like it very well. His wife didn't like the idea of his being in the Army either. I don't blame her.
*******************-

        I've written two stories in two nights for you. That makes a total of four. If you can sell them for five dollars apiece that will make twenty more dollars in the bank--which we, darlings of fortune, are discovering is not ensilage. If you can't get five dollars apiece or five dollars for the lot, I wont consider my time wasted if you apply a match to them and brew yourself a good hot cup of coffee on a cold day. Hock my sapphire cuff-links and shirt-studs and make a cafe diable.
*******************-

        Philip Wylie is my new God. Life here would be impossibly dull instead of unbearably dull if it weren't for lusty and voracious feasts on Generation of Vipers. He has excited me to all kinds of ambitiousness, and a horrible disaster will take place at my hands if I don't substitute order and truth for the bluff and reams of mis-information that has so far given me a tolerated place in polite society. AND IN YOUR NAIIVE HEART, Sweetheart. In sizing us up on Wylie's scale of adjustment to life, I am happy to report that we are two wonderfully encouraging examples of integrated Common Men. We've not completed the process--i.e. reached Tao--but we ARE killing Bogeymen right and left. We're righter than most.
*******************-

        I love myself so much more than I did before I married you. Have you noticed? That's as it should be, I think. And if this is a happy marriage, an obscure and honest little text that I've just thought up should confirm its being a happy one: Do you love yourself more now than you did before we were married?
****

        I love you, Darling--and miss you, according to the laws of Nature and Philip Wylie. I hope you have a baby.

                L*O*V*E   Kurt-

Dear Woofy:

I'll give you a gardinia when I get home--damned soon--
if you'll play Why Do I Love You--just the first part--twice
a day--but softly.

Why do I?

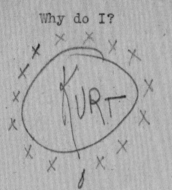

Romances Aesthetic
Are Damned Anaesthetic

Passion's
The Fashion

Kisses represented in this letter and others amount to
inflation--a damned site more than there are accumulated
in the treasury.

23 October 45

Dollbaby—

I wrote another story tonite. Honey—do me a favor and go over them for punctuation and other glaring mistakes—that is, IF they're worth saving. If they're not any good get the sons-of-bitches out of sight—and call it occupational therapy for neurotic veterans. Everybody says I can write and I say that it's a marvelous piece of intuition on their parts if it's true —because this is the first goddamn time I ever wrote. This is a very nutty world.

I am at present studying to become a person and am

173

at present staggered by the
volume of study and effort
that following demands. I
guess the current problem
before the Universe is how
to become a person as
well as feed oneself in
only eighty years of life. That's
what Guggenheim Fellowships are
for — I suppose. Let's get
one — or two, rather.
     X X X X X X X I love you,
Angel. Oh God, yes! I've got
a pang now — for all the
damn good it'll do either
of us. I hope you have
a baby. We'll know soon.
     A good guess is that
I'll be home on furlough

sometime after the 20th of November — and I'll be out for good by Christmas. That's not very far away, dear heart. Oh Golly — I swear you're perfect ——— for me.

Kurt

"
26 OCTOBER 1945
Friday........

Dollink:

                    I hate to have to thwart your proudest
ambitions for me, Angel, but I don't think I'll ever be Assistant
Cashier at the Fletcher Trust. I have decided to follow a carreer
that will keep me out in the open and on my feet--like being a floor-
walker. But office work? Jesus bless you, no. I am in an office
now, and every damned time I turn around I foul them up for the next
six weeks. I don't think I'm very bright. At least the other bright-
eyed young men in this place seem to know what's going on--guys that
haven't been here as long as I. My ambition now is to keep the rest
of the World (I feel that I owe you my confidence) from finding out that
I am not bright. We've got about fifty years of blood, sweat and
tears ahead of us. Bluffing the World for that long will not be easy.
Are you up to it? Lean on me: I have 23 years experience.

                    At which point you say, "Ah, there, but
you're not 23--yet." And I say, "True. But the time is not distant
when I Launcelot Truehart will too be 23 years of age." All of which
serves to remind me that you will remind yourself to give me something.
Well, it had damned well better not be anything a man can use in the
Army. And it had damned well better not be anything expensive. And
it had damned well better not be something that you don't want yourself.
And you'd damned well better keep it there, with you--and give it to me
when I come home in furlough some time late in November. Do I make
myself clear?

                    The first paragraph is novel subject
matter: the story of a man who wasn't bright but never knew he wasn't
bright, and by dazzling windfalls convinced the world that he was
bright--and never disillusioned himself. He never found out he wasn't
bright because he wasn't smart enough. Q.E.D.

                    Perchande I shall have a letter from you
today. At present (9:30 A.M.) I've yet to hear from you and so am
a little perturbed as to your well-being. You see, I still love you.

                    It's too damned bad we aren't equiped
with more persistant and graphic memories. The minute I loose sight
of you you stop being real to me. You stop loving me--or so it seems.
And nothing will ever convince me that you do except your actually being with me.   This is a narsty and chronic sort of torture that
haunts me all the time. I am reading War and Peace. Does that
make you happy? About my writing: mayhap I'll make myself write
another story soon. I've gone stale for a couple of days, following
a vile outburst of three stories in three nights. They were written
in the aura of a happy hangover from you. It lasted three nights and
now lies dead and ashen.

                    I'll be home between the 15th and the
20th of November. That's not far off--it says here. The 60-69
pointers start pulling stakes on the First. I still say I'll be in
flannels (legitimately) by Christmas.

                    I owe you a love letter. It will come
soon. Because I'm in love with you--that's why it'll come.

X(?)   X   X   X   X   X   X

                              Kurt

"–

26 OCTOBER 1945   9:00 P.M.
Friday

This makes six I've written:

    And you'd damned well better go over them all for spelling
and punctuation before you send them to our agent.   Mrs. Gould
once told me that stories sent to him must be perfect.   This is
the fourth story I've written in less than a week--so I think I'm
justified in thinking that I am entitled to sleep with you as a
reward.   That will I do in perhaps 20 or so days.

    I love you or I wouldn't have done this.   Whether it's
good or bad has nothing to do with it.   Good or bad it's a work
of love and somewhat pooping.

    I love you.

                    Kurt

Other works by this author include: The Rose, The Clock, The
Lunatic, The Bank Robbery, and The Hospital.

October 29, 1945

Spaniel·eyes:

On November Eleventh I want
you to do something very strange.
I want you to seclude yourself
for one-half hour in a
noiseless, distractionless place.
Do it between Nine and Nine-
thirty, P.M., Central Standard Time.
I'll be doing the same thing.
I want you to record every
thought that occurs to you
during that half-hour — Every
damned thought, Woofy, no matter
how obscure or untrue. If
they run like this: "Mephistopheles
...April...I'll Never Smile Again...
Feet hurt..." I want you
to record them. Please make
an honest effort to record

all of them—pornography and everything. We'll exchange copies and will, whether we get in telepathic phase with each other or not, have given each other a very genuine chunk of our souls. This can't fail to be at least fascinating to have side by side _exactly_ what you and I were thinking between 9 and 9:30 P.M. C.S.T. on November 11th, 1945. Not many people knew what their mates are thinking for even a split second. This idea excites me.

So do you. I'm in love with you. xxxxxxx Kurt—— (over)

At the begginning of the seance I want you to start it off with thinking — "X-ONE-NINE, X-ONE-NINE" — over and over for, say, twenty times. — then let your thoughts take you where they will. I'll do the same, starting at 9 P.M. C.S.T.

I mailed your package to you.

Happy Birthday--Dollink:
_____

        I love you most powerfully. Is this a happy birthday for you? Do
you feel as I do that we (and we couldn't do it if we were still you and I)
are on our way to an honest and blissful life? I can't get enthusiastic about
me but I go wild making plans for us. Jesus, Lamby, what one helluva lot of
fun! In sixty days or so we'll be able to BEGIN IN EARNEST. From then on
we'll be together always. We'll have lives that are ours--to have and to
hold. We'll start at Chicago--that much we know. And we'll daydream our way
from there. And I say we can't miss. Oh Golly, Dear Heart, it's not far
off. Time passes some-how. And one day soon, before Christmas, I'll be
home (that's with you) for good.

        If I timed this right it will be your birthday, and you will be
going to Phoebe's for dinner. I hope they give you a happier birthday than
I am able to do from here. If we had the price of a mink coat and not a
penny more I think you know that I'd give you the mink. Come to bed with me,
Baby, and I'll give you a mink coat--but you'll have to be patient.

        Angel, please go over the crap I've written for spelling and punct-
uation. I suppose you already have. I can picture your reading along and
suddenly looking pained; running to get a pencil to hide from the world the
astonishing gaps in the education of your loving husband. I've tried writing
stories about Germany several times--but I simply can't do it. It makes me
sick. I've forgot most of it, but part of me seems to remember and it must
have been pretty terrible. So I'm not going to try writing about Germany
again--not until I'm older.

        I'm in love with you, Woofy. I'm sure I always will be.

                                        Kurt

(Marginal doodle words: PARIS, CAPEHART, CHICAGO, HOLLYWOOD, 7 KIDS, INTELLECTUAL, BAR, (AP), PULITZER PRIZE, ROOKS, MOSCOW, HORSES, ANTHROPOLOGY, HONG KONG, PRESIDENT, BALLET, TAOS, SKIING, LONDON, CONVERTABLE, MUSIC, MAN THAT APRIL)

Woofy, wifey:

I got a long remarkable letter from a remarkable woman by the name of Hurty.   In this letter she says that she thinks both of us are pretty hot poop--which, for all I know, may be true.   In her letter she criticises what I've written.   What she days is true, dammit--mamely that if I'm going to write anything good I've got to learn something about technique.   So that's what I think I'll do--try to find out how it's done.   That, I suppose, involves work.   Send what you've got to the agent, because I don't think I'll write any more until I get home--about 17 days from today.   I don't think, in the light of Phoebe's comments, that the agent will be able to sell the stuff, but I think he'll be sufficiently fascinated to make some constructive remarks, whereupon we will make all six of the stories saleable.   Phoebe said that I xxxxxxxxx am potentially as good as Saki.   I don't believe it, but on the preposterous outside chance that she is right and I am wrong I'll give the demon that possesses me every possible opportunity.

Now then, Angel, about J.T.   I've written him a letter which he may show you (demand to see it), asking him in a nasty way to please give you a moment's peace.   If threatening notes and phone calls persist, I order you to place the following add in the Star, Times and News for one day:

ATTENTION XMAS CARD SALESMEN--J.T. Alburger will buy all the Christmas Cards that you can deliver, paying top retail prices.   Call Hu. 6224 at any time, night or day.

Simultaniously I will start a string of threatening letters to Helen.   This should get some sort of action.   I'm not kidding about the add.   Do it if he continues to heckle you.   Go downtown and put the adds in in person, paying cash on the spot.   If they want your name give them a phoney.   I find this idea extremely appealing.

Allie tells me that Jim is expected home on or about the 15th.   If this is true, Vonnegulch is going to be bedlam what with my coming home at the same time.   I'm continuing to entertain fxixxxxxx hopes, true or false, of being discharged late in November or early in December.   If anything like that does come through, we in Message Center will be the first to know of it.   For that reason I've an agreement with a friend in this office that if anything does come through while he is on furlough (Nov.2-20) I will wire xixx him about it--and vice-versa.   Not much longer, cutie, believe me. And then we'll find out how huge love can really be.   We've not been married very long--or together much.   I get starry-eyed looking ahead.   It's bound to be marvelous.

Dollink--I'm nuts about yez.

Kurt ------xxxxxx
¿?

Woofy, honey:

How?

Well, we'll have to muddle through
for a while, until we develop sufficiently; until we cease to be
infantile; until we get some sound information; until our ideas
become nails that can be driven with a hammer--instead of being
the wind-driven smoke they now are. We are young. We have
doubtless assimilated a great deal of mis-information, and there
are embarrassing gaps in our knowledge. If a bacterium can make
a man lose his judgement; if a machine can enslave a man for life;
if a labor leader can incite a dull-witted worker to smash windows;
if a mother-in-law can drive a man to drunkeness; if a prostitute
can rot the mind of a promising young man; if a brutal father can
force his children to delinquincy--then I propose that we investigate
bacteria, machines, labor leaders, mothers-in-law, prostitutes, and
brutal fathers. That will take a while.

But! Both Somerset Maugham and Philip
Wylie admit that they didn't have something REAL to write until they
were about 35. Real is right: Generation of Vipers and Of Human
Bondage. What we propose to do is a long shot. In investigation of
myself (in whom, for some damned feminine reason, you and Phoebe and
Allie have placed great hopes) I can't find much that is encouraging.
I am apparently right about a lot of things. I've a lovely set of
morals--as have you, and as have the people we give a damn about.
I'm not shrewd or clever. Right now I'm cute--and it makes me
want to vomit, thinking how cute I've been, writing for the Shortridge
Daily Echo, The Cornell Daily Sun, and now these damned short stories.
I can only hope that everyone starts out that way. I can only hope,
and this on your instigation, that I've not reached my full stature.
I'm willing to work like a dog to attain it. But, as I've heard idiots
who left school after the fifth grade say time and time again,

"Thar's plenty you won't find in books."

...The proper answer to that is, of
course, that there's an amazing plenty you will find in books, and
nothing to prevent anyone who has discovered that amazing plenty in
books from investigating that plenty you wont find in books. Our
job will be to put into books that plenty supposedly not now there.

If we go to Chicago we'll have to allow
hypocracy to support us for a while--as an underling in a Newspaper
Office or an underling in an Advertizing Office. Either one is
frankly selling one's soul to the devil. For us it's either that
or hopping rides on freights and living in Hobo Jungles. It's in
one of those two fields that I've a chance of making a living for us,
learn to write, and having adequate liesure in which to write what
seems important to us. Starting at the bottom and working up in
the newspaper business is the only prayer I've got of getting a column.

Or we could go to Mexico City, learn
the language, live the good life--and write regularly for the New
Yorker. The locality of Emily Hahn's stories is what makes them
appealing. Quaint and naiive stories from below the border may sell
like wildfire. If they're good they'll become a regular feature.
It's worth looking into, I'm sure. There we could get a perspective
on what's going on North of us. This may be the delicious angle for
which we're looking. It may be that some concern may be interested
in having a bright representative down there; willing to pay him for
a few hours work each day.

I didn't know love and marriage were
like this. I didn't know life could be this good. What I'm
realizing now are the things I dreamed as a fetus. Love...

Woofy, darling:

This is my day off. I slept until
noon and dreamed of you the whole tossing time. From time to time you've
been a Mildred to me, not in that I ever despised you, but because loving
you was so damned stinking distracting and because it made me do so many
stupid and I suppose pitiful things--despite the fact that you had told me
many times that I didn't have the chance of a snowball in Hell.   That
rotten feeling in my lungs and heart, where love and happiness also gnaw,
comes to me still.   It came to me in my dreams last night. I think that
may be one reason people grow old and disillusioned and blind to the truth.
We are built in such a way as to make it impossible to forget anything. De-
mons cannot be cast out.   I cannot bear to hear anyone speak German. Father
at dinner frequently quotes beautiful things in the original by Goethe. When
he does I recall all the beastly brutal things that can be said in that lang-
uage--and against my will project myself back to unhappier times. I'd rather
have the memory of an elephant than the memory of a man. I've the memory of
a man so I'll never be convinced that you actually love me unless I'm with you.
Darling, I've never known you before, and sometimes wonder if you knew yourself.
Angel isn't inapt--because you are an Angel.   You're the Angel that used to
come to me in my dreams, though I didn't know it was you. What I am is pretty
obvious; but the wealth of loveliness that you've shown to me is as subtle as
the Father, the Son, and the Holy Ghost.   I love you more every minute.

And that's why I'm afraid.

In the roaring, foaming, seething fury
of loving you so much I've promised and vowed and built air-castles; and beaten
my chest and torn my hair--telling what you and I would accomplish.   I get
sick with fear that I'm a bluff, that I'm actually no damned good.   That what
I've sworn to do is impossible for a person like myself. I don't know.   I have
no way of knowing.

"Can you play the violin?"
"I don't know. I've never tried."

I don't want to let you and your fantastic
hopes down with a thump.   I don't want those fantastic hopes to take the place
of love.   I don't want successes to become the consummation of that love, because
failures will be the death of it.   I want

L O V E

to exist for itself alone; separate and perfect and adequate, no matter what.
Because it's on love's account that I'm glad I'm alive.   It's on love's account
that I am willing to see life through from start to finish. Up until the time
we were married I was sorry I was alive, and, after seeing air-raid shelter
after air-raid shelter filled with dead human beings of absolutely every description, was willing to leave at any time.   I told O'Hare so several times.   He
never got to feel that way.   But I did: it's the worst feeling imaginable.

And that's why I'm afraid.

But I'm not afraid, Darling.   Because
now I remember what you are--more wonderfully loving than I thought anyone could
be.   You are the best person on Earth.   There, at last, is the answer to
the question, "Why do you love me."   Now you know why.

KURT---xxxxxx
?

Dear Woofy, wifey:

          Writing got to be a grind, and I got
to the sloppy point, before you started showing my stories to more
analytical minds, where I thought that I couldn't miss--that all I
had to do was to pound a typewriter for a couple of hours and I was
bound to come up with a winner. Well, Lamby, I pooped out. And
I was feeling fairly gruesome all day today on account of having
pooped out. BUT! Tonight I happened to read the foreign affairs
section of News Week which isn't half the charlatan that Time is.
And I read about the Russians and the Germans and the Poles and the
French and the Czechs and the Dutch and the Italians--and the fact
that people are wondering why they act the way they act--or how they
actually act, for that matter. Everything that was reported by
ace newsmen from the heart of Europe I found to be old stuff to me.
I knew intricate details like what German iron ration soup is actually
like and how much work a person can do on it;and I know what the
inside of a German box car, in which Newsweek reports thousands of
displaced persons are dying every day, looks like. I damn near died
in one myself. I know what people are crazy to know about a dozen
different nationalities--intimate things. And what I know will be
news for the next decade, because things in Europe are more unsettled
now than ever before. And those dozen nationalities are all hungry
now. And I know exactly how they act when they're hungry. And
I know how the American temperment mixes with the Czech temperment and
the Dutch temperment and the Russian temperment and the Englist temper-
ment--and any combination of the unholy goddamn mess of people that
shared hell for a while. By Jesus, I was there. That's the important thing I've got to say right now. That, by God, is xkxx why I
went through wxth what I did. I've got to say it--and at length.
You've got to make me do it and you've got to forgive and correct my
mistakes and make me see what was important about what I've seen.
You've got to ask me questions to make me remeber. It won't be a
run-of-the-mill war story--because my lousy soul isn't going to peep
once about how hungry I was or how I was mistreated. Mistreated?
Jesus, have a look at the wretched lifetime ahead of most of the
people I met over there--and look at what I've got. That's important.
And I couldn't, didn't want to write about it before, because instinct-
ively I knew that I was missing something awfully important, that anything that I would write about it would fail to reveal the SIGNIFICANT.
The name of it is going to be SCHOOL FOR DIPLOMATS. And right now I'm
in a frenzy of trying to remember every damned thing that happened.
It's going to be LONG and revealing (I'll tell the truth about the
Americans for one thing)--AND I'LL NOT BE ABLE TO DO IT WITHOUT YOUR
HELP. I'm excited, Darling, I've something to write about, something
that xdx crys out to be written. Keep this under your hat. We'll
have to talk it over before we start. We've priceless material
and a chance to do our own private set of morals a proud turn. We'll
try, by Jesus. And God bless the young. I'll have some sort of
skeleton when I get home.

          I love you Darling. Keep your shell-like
ears open for unanswered questions and popular conversation subjects
in regard to anything European. We will crawl into bed together and
make love and then we will write and then we will crawl into bed together and make love and then we will write... But while Allie is
gone you must take time out xxx to feed the dogs once a day. One
week from now..........

          XXXXX(?)

Woofy, sweety:

The main reason that I don't use too
many BIG words is that I don't know many big words.   I'll try to
write some more stories when I get home.   I'll probably do better
with you there to keep me straight.   That was a beauty about the
pipe and the hair, wasn't it?   You've surely done a sensational
job of retyping, Cookie.   I got the same thrill that Croneshaw got
when he saw his poems in print.

I'm to be payed some time soon, but
I'm not certain of getting it before I take off for Indianapolis,
and I'll not be able to do any taking off without money, so you'd
better air-mail me about twenty bucks immediately.   I plan to
pull out of this hole for the next-to-the-last-time at noon on
November 10th, Saturday.   I can't say when I'll hit Indianapolis.
Sometime on the 11th, I judge. I got the five plunks.   Spaseeba.

I like the idea of a reading club--
sort of equilibrium insurance against the constant torque of growing
old, crystaline, and complacent. These are the most horrible times
in history, I think.

Angelface: leave us not quarrel about
the Capehart.   And leave us not forget for one minute that I did
not intentionally hop all over you. This and other important matters
will be cleared up shortly.

Right now I'm groggy with the prospect
of being rudely expelled into the world. I've been examining the
shred of Persian Carpet that has so far been woven about me--and I
confess that it doesn't make much sense.   It looks more like an
honorable-mention quilt in an Iowa County Fair than a Persian
rug.   No matter.

Punk letter?   Oh well, I feel punk.
I'll be home soon.

Love...

KURT

IT IS LATER THAN YOU THINK ! ! ! ! !

SUN	MON	TUE	WED	THU	FRI	SAT
4	5	6	7	8	9	10
11	12	13	14	15	16	17
18	19	20	21	22	23	24
25	26	27	28	29	30	

LEAVE

ARRIVE

Woofykins--wifeykins:

I quote my sister: "One stipulation in a long dreamed of event: No one near when James is introduced to Jamesbo. That means simply that you and Woofy will have to go down and sit through Tarzan 20 or 30 times." So that's the way it's going to have to be.

I've found a peachy book which you must endeavor to procure, Sweety--"The Small Home of Tomorrow." I've decided that we had better start with two bedrooms. We can use one of them for a library until our union gives forth with issue. Right about the time you'll get this you'll either be feeling bloomin' lovely or bloody rum, depending upon whether our union is to be blessed with issue. Bloody rum or bloomin' lovely, Angel?

I've been fooling with time tables. I suppose it's highly idealistic of me to pay any attention to them, but the tentative schedule looks like this:

Lv Ft. Riley	4:15 PM Nov 10
Ar Kansas City	7:40 PM "
Lv Kansas City	9:00 PM "
Ar St. Louis	3:15 AM Nov 11
Lv St. Louis	9:12 AM "
Ar Indianapolis	1:46 PM "

...If that comes to pass you'll be one of the few wives on Earth that can say, "I know exactly where my husband is." Is that the way you blundered home? I have an important point to make. Give me your full attention, Dollink. DO NOT ENDEAVOR TO MEET ME. DON'T! I may miss connections, leave earlier or later than expected--or hitch-hike or do almost any damned thing. I'll call you the minute I hit town. If I haven't called you by 7 PM on November 11th, Sunday, go over to our house and wait. Pass the time by contemplating this verity: 50-point-men will definitely be eligible for discharge by, if not before, the 1st of December. It is quite possible that my furlough will be interrupted by a telegram like this:

FURLOUGH CANCELLED. REPORT TO POST FOR SEPARATION FROM ARMY.
            MUCH LOVE, COLONEL PROCTER.

I surely was excited in my last letter, wasn't I? That was last night. I was so excited that I had the screaming meemies. I've calmed down a little, now, and contemplate the titanic task proposed by myself in a more sober light. We'll start it, anyway, and see if I really have something important to tell. I get ferocious jags of ambition whenever I'm with you--and If that idea doesn't pan out we'll cook up some more that will.

I love you sweety. And if it turns out that you're going to have a baby let me tell you in advance that it will be a beautiful one: half me; half you. I repeat:
            Hello, Yin, Sweety.
            Hello, Yang, Darling.
            How are things in Tao?
            I love you, Woofy. Else why would
I bother to count the seconds and find that we are 604,800 seconds apart? Tick tock--604,799.

X X X X X X X

Did you get
your check from
Uncle S.?

K U R T

admirer, adorer, wooer, beau,
boy friend, inamorato, sweetheart,
swain, flame, love, beloved,
truelove, Lothario, amorist,
gallant, knight, cavalier servente,
cicisbeo,amoroso--Roget's

November 5th...1945

Oh Damnation, Jesus Christ, Son of a Bitch, #%$&*%#$%@#%$&*@¢!!!!!!!!!!!!!!!!!!!

This, November 5th, is the most dismally abysmal, bitterly disappointing day
of my life: fifteen minutes ago I sent you a telegram--FURLOUGH CANCELLED
INDEFINITELY. WEEP FOR BOTH OF US. Why cancelled? Oh God, it makes me
sick to write about it:--cancelled because I am essential and because Message
Center is understaffed; cancelled because there is no official way that a
replacement can be obtained for me, as I am not yet eligible for discharge.
Picture a balance in your mind: on one pan place this...

The vital importance of having me record the nature and the source of every
stupid scrap of paper to enter or leave this post;

                        and on the other place this...

I've not had a furlough in over one and a quarter years. I hate the work
and the post and am about to lose my senses. I'm not doing my job well.
I must make arrangements for entrance into the University of Chicago; locate and reserve an apartment; line up a job which I absolutely must have
if I'm to go back to school. I was promised the furlough, given the papers.
I've made wonderful plans and smiled myself to sleep over them. And then
the furlough was taken from me. My heart is broken--and it's damned well
conceivable to me that a person CAN die of a broken heart.

No--I don't know when I will be home. It's evidently none of my Goddamn
business when I see my wife.

                        "What's the matter? Don't you like it
here? Why we have movies and a library and a PX. What on earth else
do you want?"

                        I've never been so full of blind goddamn
rage. I'm off my rocker--without reason. I'm not rational. What can
I say to you?

                        You won't feel like writing letters to
me again, not after this let down. There's nothing to write about. I'm
sick at heart and probably won't write again for God knows how long. I've
been disemboweled. My guts are hanging out and little white maggots are
crawling all over them. I've had my throat slashed from ear to ear and
to all purposes I'm dead. Decayed flesh, dead and rotten.

I'm just about beaten in submission--submission to the brutal and stupid lack
of imagination on the part of those people who have God-like power, namely,
the power to RUN MY LIFE. And now they're running and ruining your life.

I've got to do SOMETHING. I'm boiling; the pressure is up and the safety
valve is inadequate; the seams are creaking and groaning.

All this because I love you and need you more than the nature of things ever
intended. That is something that cannot be explained to anyone else.

Tootles:

Last night I wrote you an air mail
letter, urging you to come out here and sweat out the discharge
with me--but I didn't mail it.   I didn't mail it because this
place is shot full of the <u>rumor</u> that the points will be lowered
to 50 before December 1st.   <u>Rumor</u> further has it that this happy
event may take place on or about November 15th.   The Army has
a reason for everything, those in command boast.   And they've
given a reason for not providing a schedule whereby a man might
predict his release.   Some damned fool General explains in the
Army Times: "When you tell a man when he's going to get out you
lose a good soldier."   In my case, a mediocre and insoucient
typist.   The fact that they might be wrecking a good civilian,
or that a good civilian is worth five tank regiments and an
aircraft carrier hasn't occured to him.   So what?   For thirty
days more at the outside I should blow my brains out, I'm esking?
I hope you're holding up all right.

I suppose we are having a dirty run of luck, but we've had a
blessed run of unbelievable, heaven-granted luck when the luck
<u>really counted.</u>   Until now, I'd forgot that was true.   I've
been crawling through this sewer for almost three years, Sweety,
an now I can see light.   What has happened to me in the Army
since we've been married strikes you as outrageous fortune.   And
it is; but it's a little outrage, Darling.   You've come in on
the tail end of it.   You came in after I'd come through the big
outrage--with two legs, two arms, and two eyes.   As you can see,
an inexplicable wave of holiness swamped me this morning, so I'll
not bitch and rant and tear my hair for a couple of days.   The
meek shall inherit the Earth, in a month or less--and then they'll
cease to be so goddamn meek.

Thus, arm in arm with you, I dare to
defy my Century to the lists.   --Schiller.   Nice?   KURT --

Yea and forsooth, my pretty little wife--Have you read the
heavenly bit of news which states that Prisoners of War with
more than 60 days in stir are to be discharged immediately?
We of Message Center have read this marvelous thing in the
Kansas City Journal and are now awaiting the official telegram from the Nation's Capital.   Capital.   This is distinctly
IT!!!!!!!!!!!!!!!!!!!!!!!!!!!!!!!!! The Sergeant Major just came
through the office, asking if any of us were Prisoners of War
and if so how long. Ha! I told him.

Jeeeheeezus, Lamby-pie. My guess is that I'll be shipped to
Atterbury in about a week, spend perhaps another week there
and I'M OUT.   That's allowing them plenty of time, an outside
estimate. Two damned lousy little weeks, Darling. We'll
buy me a grey flannel suit, ten white shirts and a dozen pairs
of sox and we're off into the big boisterous world. Holy
smokes: it's about time! No more humiliation. No more emotional suppression. Free as Hell! Picture, if you can,
what this means to me. God, what a load is about to be taken
from me. Joy. Joy. Joy. Joy. Joy. Joy.

We're off--Angel. We'll have to call a family meeting to
decide where we're going; what we're going to try to do.
We'll plan what's left of our lives to conform to our own
private set of morals, and, unlike the common man, we'll
try to plan it so we damned well WILL contribute by creating.

Be as happy as I am, Angel. This will sonn be possible:

Whither thou goest, I go; whither thou lodgest, will I lodge;
thy people shall be my people, and thy God shall be my God.

Darling wife, I love you.

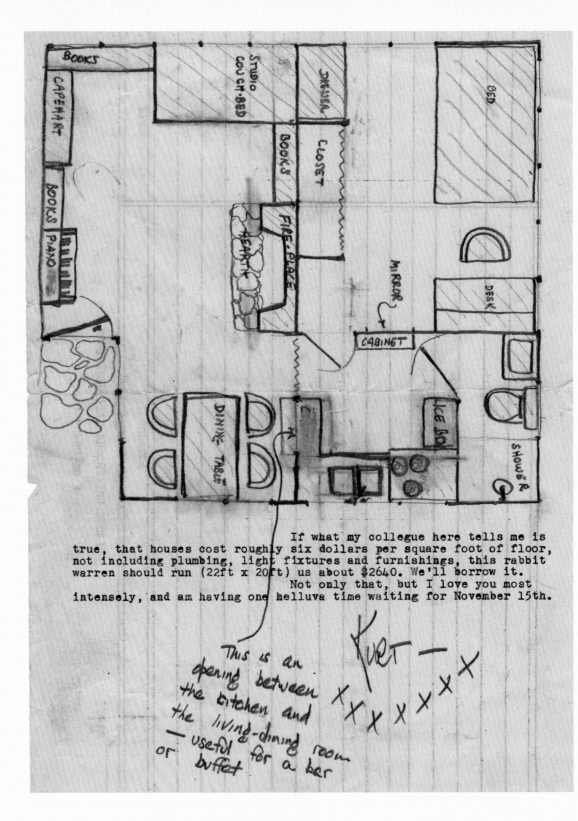

If what my collegue here tells me is
true, that houses cost roughly six dollars per square foot of floor,
not including plumbing, light fixtures and furnishings, this rabbit
warren should run (22ft x 20ft) us about $2640. We'll borrow it.
                    Not only that, but I love you most
intensely, and am having one helluva time waiting for November 15th.

Kurt —

X X X X X X X

This is an
opening between
the kitchen and
the living-dining room
— useful for a bar
or buffet

S-w-e-a-t-i-n-g   i-t   o-u-t:

I'm waiting for the OFFICIAL word, Angel.   It is 8:30 P.M., Thursday.
Another batch of telegrams is due in here shortly; the last batch of
the night.   A replacement for me has been requisitioned--so I know the
BIG NEWS is likely to break at any minute.   Jesus, when?   Methinks
in twenty-four hours or less.   Holy smokes: talk about being tense.
Sleeping is out of the damned question.   Maybe I'll be out in a week?
Or less?   A possibility.   Things were a damned sight better than we
thought, eh?

Scammon Lockwood is exciting--I'll say that for him.   He sounds like
something out of Popular Mechanics, doesn't he?   He's surely well-
oriented in the world of machines.   If I show any promise I think he'll
give us a big boost to where we want to go.   I'm fairly convinced that
he's not a phoney--aren't you?   What we need is professional advice
and an in with the editors.   He can give it to us, I think.   Young and
inexperienced as I am, our primary purpose for the present should be to
MAKE MONEY while I learn to write.   If I can get shrewd and prolific
enough to turn out a steady flow of frivolous slush in exchange for a
steady flow of hard cash I'll certainly throw myself into the job with
all my heart.   Witness Philip Wylie and his fishing series.   We'll
keep and nourish bigger ideas until we're older--and one helluvalot more
skilful, and truthful--i.e. accurate.

Right now love is the biggest thing--the thing to nourish: because it's
the thing that can make us most genuinely, thuroughly happy.   That's
what I'm coming home to.   That's the basis; that's the foundation on
which we'll be free to build in a few short days.   Golly, you're a
heavenly person, Woofy.   I love you, Darling.   I will eat you up....
....in a minute or two.   Tick tock.   Wait.   We're on the THRESHOLD.
I love you, Darling.   Tick tock.

KURT
xxxxxxx (OVER)

```
FOR THIS IS THE VERY ECSTASY OF LOVE                     Sunday afternoon--11 November 45
WHOSE VIOLENT PROPERTY FORDOES ITSELF
AND LEADS THE WILL TO VIOLENT UNDERTAKINGS.  -Hamlet
```

Beloved:-

       Still no news. I've spent the bulk of these past few days--now that the end is in sight--staring at the ceiling, trying to figure out how I'll spend the vast remainder of my days. And I've spent the bulk of these past few nights dreaming of the sparkling little lake of heavenly nights we've spent together and of the turquoise ocean of them that lies before us. The nocturns are lush and loving, warm and splendid--but the day dreams are obscure, clouded. I wonder....

       Rich man, poor man, beggar man, thief? Doctor, Lawyer, Merchant, Chief? From your loving me I've drawn a measure of courage that never would have come to me otherwise. You've given me the courage to decide to be a writer. That much of my life has been decided. Regardless of my epitaph, to be a writer will have been my personal ultimate goal.

       What must I do to become a writer? From what I know about authors--Mencken, Lewis, Sinclair, Wylie, Wells, Farrel, Lardner, Hecht--most of them are products of the advertizing and newspaper worlds. Of those I've named, none gives much credit to Universities for their successes. By and large they were born to write--and most of their information has been picked up through a voracious appetite for books. Wylie is the most noteworthy collector of extraneous information. So I think I'll serve an apprenticeship in an advertizing concern--Leo Burnett's, if he'll have me. Under the G.I. Bill of Rights we'll have tuition, fees and books paid for, with an additional $90 per month for living expenses. That, obviously, is not adequate--far from it. The necessity of establishing myself as a valuable and fairly well-paid family head is important. If I go to the University of Chicago, I will be 25 or 26 years old by the time I finish the anthropology course we're considering having me take. I am going to give Chicago a try for a year. But sweety, in spite of the fact that we'll be bucking the iron-clad middle class prejudice against men without degrees, if I decide I'm getting no damned or very little benefit from my studies I'm going to chuck them. I'll go to work as a full time reporter or copy writer. I think it's the _soundest_ way to gain our end--and lucrative as well.

       We want to end up with a sydincated daily column or a writing job in Hollywood or as a playwright or as a novelist. Or a brick layer, or a beach comber, or a merchant seaman, or a street cleaner. But we'll have tried.

       I love you, **Angel**. We'll take turns putting our heads on each other's beloved tummies and talking things over. By the time you get this you'll have only a short time to wait--hours, maybe. Darling, I'm a humorless and thick bastard from time to time--of that I'll say more when I get home. People are walking contradictions: I've noticed it in myself recently. I'll stop it when love resumes its three dimensions instead of two--the length and width of this piece of paper.

Love lieth deep; love dwells not in lip depths.

                                      Kurt
                                         X X X X X X X

November 12th--Monday night
1945

Dear Heart:

        This is akin to torture, this waiting.   This is the
most sterile life imaginable: an insipid broth concocted of ten
parts working, ten parts sleeping, two parts eating, three parts
movies, and ten parts sitting--wondering what in Hell is behind
it.   I have two days off each week, but I'm damned if I wouldn't
rather work every day to make the time go faster. I've a bald and
baseless hunch that tomorrow is the day that orders for my release
will come through. If the orders do come, the train ride to Atterbury
will follow in a couple of days.

        I've done quite a nice job of delivering Wylie-esque
lectures these last two days to the dull, the sloth and the thunder-
struck who sleep in the barracks with me.   This marks the first
time I've opened my yap to my dim-witted companions since I got
here in October.   It all started with a Troglodyte's allowing as
how he would like a television set when he gets out.   It was like
shooting fish in a rain barrel.   I led the poor dupe to doom by
asking him why he wanted a television set. I'd learned my lesson
well.   There wasn't an undangled jaw in the place as I closed my
passionate case against the world of gadgets which the cave men
most of us are have come to think of as marvelous progress.

        All of which reminds me that I am not infallible, Cookie,
and that I would do well to keep my ears open for homely wisdom that
those who have actually bucked the world can give me.   As you know,
I haven't bucked the world as yet.   This is one thing I learned this
apres midi--from a graduate lawyer.   "Right after I got out of
Law School (St. John's) my wife and I got to thinking.   We decided
that if a man makes his living in a profession--Doctor, Lawyer, Dentist, Architect--he's going to be making his living with his hands.
If something happens to him or his hands--I don't care if he's making
a million a year--his money's going to stop coming in.   If something
goes wrong with him, he and his family are going to be in a very
tough spot indeed.   That's why my wife and I opened a fruit store
in Rockway Beach.   Christ, I've got four of the damned things now,
and even while I'm here in the Army I'm getting a sweet income from
them. In a couple of more summers, once I'm discharged, I'll be able
to retire--at 35!"

        ...Which makes me think that our Library-Bar might well
be worth looking into, Sweety.   If, in a couple of years, we do
open a bar, it won't be denying our original aims--it'll simply serve
to augment them.   Perchance security in the face of dubious artistic
endeavor.   Besides, I rather fancy myself in the role of Mine Host.
We'll supervise it for a while and then get someone else to run the
joint.   We stand a blissful chance of wringing a great deal of pleasure out of life, fifteen minutes of which have ebbed since I started
this letter.   Remind me to study the New Testament in the light of
what Wylie said about him. I think we stand to learn a lot by doing
so.   That, I think, comes under the heading of Unitarianism.

        I love you, Angelface.   I told you so earlier today.
Jim must be home by now, and has probably spirited my sister off to
McCormack's Creek.   Love, of which you as my wife have taught me
every heavenly thing I know, is stupifying in its importance. Love,
as you have shown it to me, is astonishing, overwhelming.   Love
is a blissful rhythm of joyously hopeful days and moist and billowing
nights.   Thank God we're as young as we are, Darling, and thank
him for making us so much in love with each other.
- -
SAVE THIS VALUABLE COUPON!!!!!!!!!!!!
                        This coupon entitles the bearer to one-thousand,
seven-hundred and twenty-eight loving kisses, to be bestowed, one
each, on every square inch of her beautiful body.
                              Kurt Vonnegut, Jr.

November T*H*I*R*T*E*E*N*T*H* 1945
Tuesday evening....................

Dearest Woofy:

          At long last, Wife, I've discovered that
this waiting we're having to do is another piece of rotten luck,
the likes of which has pursued me for the whole of my Army life.
Camp Funston is the location of AGFRD#3, a sub-division of
greater Fort Riley. I've just learned that the last of the 50
pointers and P.W.'s at Fort Riley proper were discharged today--
because they are members of SURPLUS units.   I am not a member
of a surplus unit and consequently cannot leave this stinking
place until a replacement is obtained for me.   That, Dear Heart,
is the horrible reason for the orders for P.W. releases not having
come down!   Put that in your pipe and smoke it.   I've been
sucking on this bitter briar filled will smouldering horseshit
for three years.   I wont be held up much longer--no more than
a livid ten or fifteen days--on account of it.   BUT IT MAKES ME
SO GODDAMNED MAD.   JESUSCHRISTGODALMIGHTYDAMNSONOFABITCHINGBULL
SHITTINGBLUETESTICLEDSTINKINGFATASSEDPIMPOFAHOMOSEXUALONENUTBASTARD.
...And the pure hell of it is that this is a dry State!

          If I don't write for a while it wont be because
I'm on my way home and it wont be because I've stopped loving you.
It'll be because I'm so damned upset that I can't make myself sit
in one place long enough to write a letter, and because my mind is
so addled that I can't.   That last sentence, I'm afraid, isn't
quite right, but you get the drift of it, I think.

          Find out about a place for us to live in
Chicago.   I'll call you from Atterbury if I ever get there.   And
if I'm not home by George Washington's Birthday write Harry Truman
a nasty letter.

          JEEEEEEEEEEEEEEEHEEEEEEEEEEZUS, I'M BURNING UP!

          You will get this on Friday, November 15th.
Don't let this letter upset you, Sweety.   Because by Friday
things may be of a far lovelier complexion--and this is merely an
amusing record of how I felt three days ago.

          I love you.   When the big news breaks it'll
come quickly.   We've got the unbelievable bliss of its reception
still ahead of us.   People talk of the happiest times of their
lives.   That will be among the happiest times of my life!   But
without a doubt the happiest times in my life have been spent in
bed with you.   That is the absolute peak of joy--and we'll soon
have it every night.   Why do people stay single?   Probably because what we've got is brewed of love.   A lot of people never
get a sniff at it.

          Love love love love love love love

                    KURT

Tell me, Spaniel-eyes, would you like to matriculate in the University of Mexico in Mexico City--instead of going to Chicago? I corresponded with them three years ago, when I was planning to quit Cornell and go there. I was called to Duty instead. Just for the hell of it I'm going to write them again as I've forgotten the details of their plans for Americans.

You and Phoebe surely gave me the works. I stand properly rebuked and resolved to do better--If it kills me. But can you understand that I cannot bring myself to do anything, leave alone anything good, here? This is the most dismal life imaginable. It's the most depressing. It will be that way until I'm whole again. From reveille to taps I'm an oaf, a clown, a hulk. I am flesh; heavy flesh that must be dragged from place to place. It responds to heat and pressure and pain. That's what it responds to.

Don't poop yourself out typing up my stories, Sweety. They're not worth it. They are exercises and not much more. Exercises for what we both hope will be something amazingly good. I've an awful lot to say, Sweety, in response to your awe-inspiring letters. But let it wait a while--17 days.

Please, Angel, send me five-bucks (if you haven't already) by air mail, as I haven't the price of a coke or a movie.

I wish I could write as well as you. Right now you're the composer and I'm the musical instrument. We periodically swap roles.

I'm blissfully married, Darling. Be patient with me, Woofy, and keep in mind that I've been asleep for almost three years. I'm seeing the world through the eyes of Rip Van Winkle. Do you understand that all of this is NEW to me; that on every page of every book I read and in every kiss is a revelation? I'm amazed and staggered, Sweety. Be patient.

KURT

P.S. Practically everyone here thinks that I am a nut. This is highly encouraging.

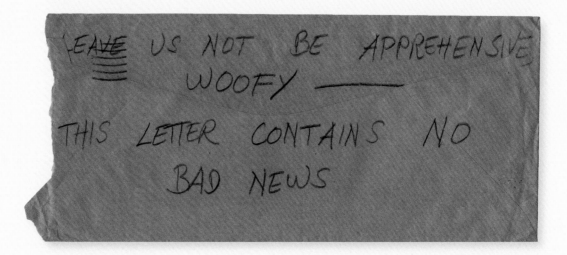

Dear Wife:-

It happens to every couple, naturally--this business of
the marriage marking major emotional and intellectual shakeups and
realignments. But the products of our particular adjustment are
hellish exciting. Apart from the fabulous pleasures in bed--the
blessed bliss of which I'd never expected or experienced--an amazing
collection of hopes and ideas has spontaniously (at least on my
Rip Van Winkle part) demanded, and will get, our attention.

........Darling, you've written remarkable letters this past month.
After reading them I feel like kicking myself for having sent you
the infantile mass of crap most of my letters are.

I've finished a fiendishly revealing book on psychiatry,
the first of its sort that I've ever read: The Human Mind--by Dr.
Karl Menninger. Reading it has startled me into recognizing
some things about myself, motives; it has shredded several cherished
falsehoods, thrown light into obscure corners--and given me a
million ideas as to what I should write about, and as many accurate
plots (case histories) to go with them. I think we'd better buy it.
No other book ever hit me this hard before.

........All of which leads me to wonder. Just how shrewd an analyst are you, Angel? I realize now that my letters to you are almost
dreamlike in their wandering lack of inhibition--and to anyone with
an inkling of psychiatric theory, my aimless symbolism and imagery
would illuminate my befouled mental sewers. Methinks you've been
uncommonly shrewd.

...Take my wanting you to open up and engulf me...Take my
attachment to Aunt Edna and Phoebe...Take their enthusiastic return
of it...Take your outspoken maternal instinct...Take your unquestion-
ing love of your father...Take your occasional outbursts against your
mother...Take my baseless distrust of my father...Take the fact that
you and I have almost gravitated together into marriage...Take the
fact that we share a love that seems unreasonable in its magnitude
at times...   This retrospection shows nothing abnormal. It
does, I think, give a true picture of our motives--which mesh perfectly, giving the classic picture of Ying and Yan. It explains and
confirms the happy ending. Or the happy beginning.

* *

I wonder if you are going to have a baby. We'll get you
a pregnancy test when I get home. When will I get home? Oh Dammit,
Angel, I still don't know. The orders haven't come down yet. Everyone, including the officers, expected them to come down yesterday.
Believe me--they can't hold them up much longer. We've been going
through a dismaying series of broken promises. It has been rough on
me and I suppose a thousand times as rough on you. It wouldn't
surprise me if that were the cause of your uneasy little tummy. I
love your tummy.

I'm afraid one requisite of being a full fledged and accredited
intellectual is an astounding scholastic record. You have one. I don't.
And I doubt if I'll ever have one. I can't explain it, but I'm not
academically worth a damn.   Another requisite is a string of advanced
degrees. My record is not encouraging in that august direction, and
I've neither the time nor the money to pursue them. Sweety, we'll
have to blunder our way into World respect through channels other than
those followed by Stringfellow Barr and Milton Mayer. I think we
have a chance of doing it--despite your devoted husband's painfully
evident short-comings--by starting with "Compassion is the first if
not the only law of human existence," and by reading until we're blind,
talking things over until our teeth fall out, writing until our hands
are hamburger, and staying madly in love until Hell freezes over.

Your perfect letter has made me think of hundreds of things,
Dear Heart. One day soon we'll exchange the things we've been saving.

DEAR WIFE:

Let's talk about something pleasant for a change. My perpetually being on the brink of despair is childish: there's no real reason for my being a gloomy and bitching Gus when this foolish story that took three years to tell has practically come to THE END.

If we're to set up a home: if we're to fly the nest properly; if we're to establish our individual dignity as Mr. and Mrs. Kurt Vonnegut, Jr.—then we'd better start thinking about money. We think we've got remarkable minds: they'll be tested presently for World-worthiness.

FOOD: In speaking with several of my married collegues I've discovered that it is entirely possible to feed two people for a week for $12 to $15. I gather that this amount, properly adminstered will do the job nicely.

SHELTER: We'll have to find out what apartments cost in Chicago. Didn't the Boorstons say something about $50-$75 per month? Get Ruth Lieber to land us an apartment if I'm not home by December 10th. If, through outrageous fortune, I'm not home by then you may have to go to Chicago and pick out home without me.

CLOTHING: My discharge pay will fit me out satisfactorily. Dear Heart, of what apparel are you in need?

ASSETS: Tuition and $75 a month ($90 pending legislation) from the great white-bearded idiot; about $800 in the bank; a mess of bonds I haven't counted; $20,000 in securities on which we can and will borrow. Financially that's it. Spiritually we've promise of a great deal more. Sweety, we'll have to borrow to give ourselves a boost.

I'm not worried. Don't you be worried either. I can hardly wait to get started. If it weren't for loving you I wouldn't feel this way.

XXXXXX

KURT

Saturday night--November 24th
1945

WIFE DARLING:

I'm not very glib this evening--probably because I think
I've something to say for a change.

Primarily, I think it's this:--
The time is not distant that we'll be reunited, and that
reunion will actually mark our being married. We've had thirty
turgid days together, Darling, during which we've set a dozen beds
to creaking and groaning with the unfathomable delights of making
love to each other. I hope we continue to make beds complain for
the next fifty years, Beloved, at the end of which heavenly time
we dry up simultaniously--sleeping peacefully in twin beds, each
with a high regard for the brains of the other. Sweety, to date
we've been lovers. In a week or less from the time you get this
we'll be man and wife--a new situation. My first night home will
be our wedding night (and I'll probably act it!). From then on
we'll be together for the rest of our lives. Our being married
will have some meaning. And when we die let's hope the same will
be said for our lives. That's the big thing: we'll be free to make
our lives significant as well as happy. If we are both charred
beyond recognition in the Atomic War, let's die with the assurance
that IF any life survives us we will have left some little nucleus
of truth or goodness on which the scorched survivors may build.
These are the most colossal times in history. Man has evidently
released a source of energy from within himself that is overpowering--
subtle, insidious. Decay. Resignation, rot. Suicide. Carbon-
monoxide: tasteless, colorless, odorless.

Application blanks for discharge of men with 55-60 points
were distributed today. I filled one out and turned it in. I
have 57 points. Nothing has been said about the P.O.W.'s, but
the men in the above point group are to be released starting on
December 1st. I have my replacement so nothing is likely to hold
me up. The P.O.W. release announcement was a filthy trick on the
part of the War Department, to make the bamboozled citizenry think
that demobilization was going a great rate. I'll be home by the
fifth easily, Angel. I'll telegraph when I know for sure. We'll
stay in Indianapolis until I can get some clothes and then toddle up
to Chicago. If I'm not mistaking, poor Wife, you will be in a sad
condition for my homecoming. We'll wait until you get over that be-
for we go home hunting.

Answer this letter immediately by air mail. It will be
the last letter you'll ever have to write to your loving husband...

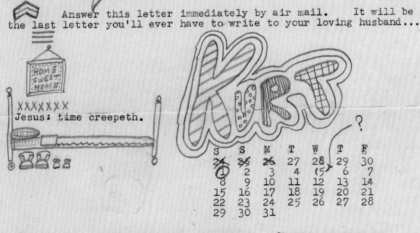

XXXXXXX
Jesus: time creepeth.

S	S	M	T	W	T	F
24	25	26	27	28	29	30
1	2	3	4	(5	6	7
8	9	10	11	12	13	14
15	16	17	18	19	20	21
22	23	24	25	26	27	28
29	30	31				

GOLLY BUT I LOVE YOU A LOT, SWEETHEART. ♡ ♡ ♡ ♡ ♡ ♡

```
JOYJO'
BLISSE
ECSTAS'
HEAVE
DELIG
SPLEN'
FUNFU
LOVELO
JOYJO'
BLISSE
ECSTASY
HEAVENF
DELIGH
SPLENI
FUNFUN
LOVELO
JOYJOYJ
BLISSBI
ECSTAS
HEAVEN
DELIGHT
SPLENDE
FUNFUNI
LOVELO
JOYJOY.
BLISSBL
ECSTASY
HEAVEN
DELIG'
SPLENI
FUNFUN
JOYJO'
```

December 1st, 1945
Saturday Afternoon

Dear Wife:

Periodically, in a cycle that I will
one day for the helluvit graph, I go completely off my unstable nut--on a jag of hitching my little red wagon to big
silver stars. It happened to me again last night. Reading
an unusually stimulating issue of LIFE (the one that raises
Hell with Indianapolis) set me off. I wanted to be another
Bennett Cerf and I wanted to be a top drawer diplomat and I
wanted to be an ace motion picture director and I wanted to
be a playwright and I wanted to be another Spencer Tracy.
Patient and Beautiful Wife, the slightest stimulus will
and always has set my roulet-wheel mind whirling around the
"Rich man, poor man, beggar man, thief--Doctor, Lawyer, Merchant, Chief..." axis. 'Round and 'round she goes, and where
she stops, nobody knows.

Beloved Wife, methinks you're not overly
fond of my parapitetic ambitions. Sweet wife, I am that way
because I'm fascinated by the remarkable lot of good and delight-
ful work there is to be done on Earth. Also, I am passionately
worshipful of competance. I love and respect intellectual
authority. I have been a constant antithesis of intellectual
authority as a perfectly rotten student. Now I want to be a
mental big shot myself, and, bottled up in the Army as I have
been, I've not had a chance to take much of an academic step
in any direction. So, Ooomph Girl, I've been like a Brooklyn
tenement dweller thumbing through a seed catalogue. "If I
had a garden I'd plant these Rosalinda Gladiolas, with a border
of Amsterdam Velvet Tulips--or maybe these Lord Dudley Zinnias
would look better...etc."

Whatever the outcome, Anthropology will
be the foundation. The more I think about it the more pleased
I am with the choice of the course of study. Dear Heart, it
entails my going to school until I'm 26. During these next
three years I'm going to be making assaults on fame and income
in every way I can think of. I'm looking foreward to a
heavenly time the rest of my life because I love you so much,
Wife.

Sweety, I gather that no one but father
is now living at Vonnegulch. When I come home I imagine that
it will be in the afternoon, though I don't know by what means
I'll come. I'll come straight to Williams Creek--and I'd
like you to be there when I arrive. That is selfish of me,
I suppose, but that's what I'd like. So, we'll revise the
code a little. You'll get the telegram on the day prior to
my arrival. If it says UNCLE LOUIS DIED THIS MORNING AND
LEFT A COOL MILLION be at Vonnegulch in the morning. Oh
what the hell, Angel. I must be off my rocker with the excite-
ment. I'll send you a straight wife or call you up to give
you the dope.

I love you...............veddy much.

XXXXXXX
P.S. Tomorrow I leave Fort Riley forever. I report to Fort
Leavenworth Monday morning. That, Dear Heart, is when the
marvelous business of separating me from the goddamned service
begins.

—

Love, Woofy

...

IN ALL MY SEARCHING, I FOUND ONLY ONE LETTER FROM MY mother to my father during this time, as well as one letter she wrote on his behalf to a literary agent.

It shows so clearly how essential she was in encouraging, editing, and guiding Kurt with her unswerving belief in him. She saw his potential before any other and she constantly advocated for him. He just needed a little direction and cleaning up, like a diamond in the rough.

It is very important to me that my mother be given her proper place in my father's writing trajectory. She never would have claimed it for herself. As her daughter, I am pleased to step in and deliver the evidence so there is no question of her contribution. She had some of the best qualities a person can have. She listened, supported, and nurtured with all her heart and soul. She devoted her life to helping this man. I see often that this is what some women do. They support and give their lives over to helping another. It's beautiful and maddening at the same time.

Darling---

It is GOOD!!!!!!! Sweety, Love, it is a jewel, a gem; you are
wonderful!!! Darling, I just don't know how you do it.. There's nothing
wrong with it, it's PERFECT.. You couldn't have done better if you had had
umpteen trillions of courses in short story writing.. Sweety, I married a
GENIUS... That is all there is to it... I feel the way I did when I discovered how wonderful Chekhov is---- only this is you, and I just can't believe it,
I can't, I can't, I can't... But it's TRUE... Oh, my love, I am completely and
utterly overcome, I don't know when I've been so excited, I'm shaking.. Mother
is reading it now, and then I'm taking it to Allie to read right away...
Sweetheart, let me try to tell you why I'm so awfully excited--- I always
knew you could Write-- but suddenly I am finding out that you seem automatically
to Know technical details about form and exposition, and so forth, that most
people have to spend years reading books and taking correspondence courses
to find out, and then they can't do it ... Phoebe and I were just talking
about it last night--- how hard it is to achieve all the little tricks that
are necessary to any particular form of writing in order to make it SELL..
A good short story is an awfully hard thing to write-- there's so much
you have to put in it, and so much you have to leave out.. You've never
written a short story, and now suddenly you write one, and there's nothing
wrong with it ... Sweets, it too astounding to believe... You've got just
the right words in just the right places; your description is perfect, you
know how to wind it in and around the dialogue, which is also perfect ; the
way you have made the emphasis fall as much on the character and lifetime of
the ice-man as on the story of the rose-- for the story of the rose serves as
much to bring him out as he brings it out-- is a master-stroke, darling, which
never occurred to me.. The feud between the two ladies is beautifully done;
and the tie-up between the characters, including you and me, is clear-cut and
subtle at once.. Have you read A Portrait of the Artist as a Young Man?? You
must.. Anyway, in that, Stephen Dedalus, talking of Art, quotes Aquinas:
" Ad pulcritudinem tria requiruntur integritas, consonantia, claritas.....
Three things are needed for beauty, wholeness, harmony and radience." You
have created a things of beauty, my love, for that little story has those
three things, wholeness, harmony and radience.. Darling, I am firmly convinced
that you are the best writer on the face of the earth today. I know it. I

don't know much, but I know that.. You're not as good as Chekhov yet, simply
because you haven't said anything of as much importance-- But you know HOW
to say it, and as time goes on, you'll have more and more of it to say.. You
write as well as any short story writer I have ever read... I am so proud
of you I want to EXPLODE...

Allie thought it was wonderful; so did Mother and Daddy. Monday I am going
to take it to Phoebe? because she is frightfully, frightfully interested and
she knows how good you are too.. Phoebe and I had a most interesting talk
about you and writing and me and books and her and writing and writing and
writing.. She is going to give me a little book with some of the rulds in
it.. She says you have already read it......

I love you, I love you, I love you........

Now, I am going to call Mrs. Gould and get the name of that agent.. June
Brown is no good because she is only interested in selling her own things and
won't like the idea of someone else using her agent .. There is no point at
all in wasting any more time without an agent-- he would be SURE to sell it.
It is New Yorker, dear, not Atlantic Monthly or Esquire... It is New Yorker
more than anything else...

I love you, I love you, I love you...

WRITE more, dear.. WRITE? WRITE, WRITE... You are tremendously good, believe
me... You are out ofthis world you are so tremendously good...

I feel more happy, enthusiastic, inspired, excited, blissful than I have
since you left... You make me so awfully happy, darling... I love you...

Woofie

X X X X X X

207

November 7, 1945

Indianapolis,
Indiana

Dear Mr. Lockwood;

Thank you for your prompt answer to my query. I am enclosing
four of my husband's short stories. There are more, but I don't want
to send them until we hear what you have to say about these.

In answer to the request in your booklet for personal information: My husband is ▓▓▓nty-three years old, and is at present
leading a stagnant life as a corporal at Fort Riley, Kansas. He was
born and raised in Indianapolis. He attended Cornell University,
where he was a moderately successful misfit in Bio-chemistry but spent
most of his time writing for the Cornell Daily Sun, of which he became
Managing Editor in his Junior year. He enlisted in the Army before
he entered his Senior year and spent the next two years and a half
pursuing the usual undistinguished career of a private in the Infantry,
the climax of which was his capture last December in ▓▓▓ Battle of the
Bulge. He was a prisoner of war for six months in Dresden -- concerning
which dreadful experience he has a long and potentially remarkable
article in mind, and which he intends to write after he is discharged.
He was liberated by the Russians in May, returned home, regained some
fifty-odd pounds, became engaged to me in July, and married me on
September 1st. We are very happily married, in case that has anything
to do with it. Since everyone tells him he can write, he is now
writing.

As for our literary aims -- both his and mine -- they are so
high as to be at this point a little absurd. I personally am convinced
that he is a potential Chekhov, and as soon as he's lived long enough
to have something worth saying, he'll prove it. My opinion, I cannot
resist adding, is not to be disregarded as the half-baked prejudice
of a fatuous ▓▓▓ng newly-wed, please. I may be very ignorant, as

my husband repeatedly tells me, about a lot of things, but about writing I'm not. Swarthmore College, liberal institution that it is, graduated me with high honors and gave me Phi Beta Kappa for no other reason than that I was able to prove I knew good writing when I saw it. I am passing along this inconsequential bit of information for the frank purpose of impressing you. As far as I can see, Phi Beta Kappa isn't good for anything else, and just now we need terribly to impress someone.

But I was talking about our literary aims. I am taking the liberty ████████ sending you one of his latest letters to me. It is in answer to one of mine asking how we are going to help cure the World of Evil (that's how young we are). I think he can speak better for himself than I can for him, and this letter contains the kernel of his thinking about our Future, and also a few motley ideas on which you may have some commentary. I want the letter back, please. If we hadn't been so recently married, my sending it to you could be grounds for divorce; but things being as they are, I think I'm safe.

As I hope you will be able to divine from the letter, he doesn't want to write drivvle; he wants to say something important. The idea in brief is that, when we die, we want the world to be a little bit better in some respect or other, than it was when we were born, on account of (among other things) what we did and said while we were alive. And the only mode of expression which we feel congenial is writing. I realise that that is a big order, but you asked for it, and you got. I think that he considers what he has written so far pure drivvle. It is -- if you're looking for tremendously Significant subject matter ████████ on the other hand, one of the stories has an idea that will make people stop and think (if it's printable; I doubt that it is), and the others have a warmth of expression and characterization that is appealing even if it isn't exactly important.

The motivation behind these stories is our current philosophy
that the end justifies the means. Just now we need money; we haven't
got anything but the G.I. Bill of Rights, and you can't live the
good life on that. If you can sell these to any magazine, no matter
how pulpish, we'll not be snotty. I do not honestly believe that they
are pulp material, but then I don't know anything about the pulps.
They haven't enough plot, and aren't sexy, adventurous, glamorous, or
even long enough for such magazines as the Saturday Evening Post,
Redbook, the Cosmopolitan, and so on. My untutored opinion is that
they are suitable for the New Yorker, Esquire, the Atlantic, and
magazines of that general class.

About these fees. Does the reading, criticising and selling
of a manuscript cost $3.00, plus 10% commission, and postage, which
we are able to pay? Or is some one of the three Plans compulsory to
your getting the stories sold? Because, if it is, we can't afford
you. We are both going to the University of Chicago when he is
discharged, which will be shortly; there we are somehow going to have
to live on $75.00 a month, plus the meagre Fellowship which I have a
prayer of getting. You can easily see that we won't have either $10.00,
or $15.00, or $20.00 left over. Sorry.

I am anxious to hear your reaction to all this.

Sincerely yours,

We wish you a Happy New Year!

ADAMS * VONNEGUT *

Nan Peter Steve Jim Edie Mark Tiger

BEYOND 1945

IN THESE LOVE LETTERS, KURT REPEATEDLY STATES THAT he wants seven children. Kurt and Jane got the seven children, but not the way they intended.

On September 15, 1958, Kurt's sister, Allie, and her husband died within thirty-six hours of each other, the result of breast cancer and a freak train accident. They left behind four boys, ages two, nine, eleven, and fourteen. Our little family of five grew to nine overnight. I was eight at the time, my sister four, our brother eleven. Despite the sudden, horrific tragedy, we became a wonderfully quirky, close family. My mother, known as "Aunt Jane" to all our friends, was the warm center of our home, in which the orphaned nephews were able to recover from their devastating loss, and my brother and sister and I were allowed to flourish. She took care of all of us, including Kurt, exquisitely, with the most open, kind heart I have ever known in a human being.

For Jane, there was nothing as tangible as a book or painting to show at the end of the day. In addition to recognizing that Kurt was going to become a great writer and helping him get there, her hours were spent doing all the things that aren't usually considered evidence of a brilliant life worth examining: the endless laundry, grocery shopping, meals, dentist appointments, after-school activities, and baking of birthday cakes (it was always someone's birthday). She created the messy, loving environment through which we could all swerve in and out, and our off-the-wall fun house was where all our friends wanted to be. Jane allowed us to congregate and carry on in large numbers, but kept us from the room where Kurt worked. During these tumultuous, broke years, from 1958 to 1969, he wrote *The Sirens of Titan; Mother Night; Cat's Cradle; God Bless You, Mr. Rosewater; Welcome to the Monkey House;* and *Slaughterhouse-Five.*

After the publication of *Slaughterhouse-Five* and the fame that followed, Kurt left Jane in 1971.

My parents talked frequently and easily after their divorce. Kurt moved to New York and remarried. Jane had been hurt but never became bitter. In 1986, I was with my mother as she was dying from ovarian cancer at the age of sixty-four. She asked me to ring up Kurt. She was too weak to dial or hold the phone. When he answered, I said, "Dad, Mom wants to talk with you" and lifted the phone to her ear.

Their voices were soft and intimate. They were profoundly alone with each other. I was merely the phone-holder, but I heard. She said, "Kurt, I need to go. Do you have any idea how I can leave this ruined body?" He replied, "Okay, listen, close your eyes and take a walk down to the end of the lane to Barnstable Harbor. It's high tide. A beautiful, clear blue, calm summer day. The water is smooth like glass. There is a boy. He picks up a small, flat, smooth stone. Watch him skip that stone across the water. Watch as the stone skips and skips and goes slower and slower and further and further. When the stone stops and finally sinks, that's when you can go." Jane thanked him, they said they loved each other, and that was the last time they spoke. She died seven days later.

IT'S BEEN AN ODD and fascinating project to wedge myself into these pages from my father to my mother. It reminds me of something my father once said while teaching writing in Iowa City. He told his students, "All you can do is tell what happened. You will be thrown out of this course if you are arrogant enough to imagine that you can tell me why it happened. You do not know. You cannot know."

I can never know why my parents' love story ended the way it did. But now, at the age of seventy, I have an extraordinary bird's-eye view of the time compressed in these letters between two kids in their twenties, grappling with raging hormones, A-bomb fears, and impossibly grand expectations. They pledged to each other to try to leave the world better than they found it. Turns out, they did.

—EDITH VONNEGUT

ACKNOWLEDGMENTS

I'D LIKE TO THANK my editors, Caitlin McKenna and Emma Caruso, at Penguin Random House. Our entire working relationship has been through emails and phone calls. At this writing, we have not yet met in person. However, when I try to imagine them, I see fierce young Katharine Hepburn types. They shepherded me every step of the way to making this collection of letters as good as it could possibly be. Sometimes they felt like empathetic sisters and sometimes they felt like kindly grammar teachers. The final months of work were accomplished during the coronavirus's assault on New York City, March and April of 2020. They simply kept soldiering on without missing a beat.

I'm eternally grateful to Kristina Moore at the Wylie Agency who initially brought this project to the attention of Random House, and to my agent, Katie Cacouris, who has been alongside me this whole time in the best way.

Huge thanks to Meera Subramanian and Steve Prothero, real writers who gave me real support early on.

To my husband, John, who is the quiet strong center of my life.

And finally to my father for writing these letters and to my mother for keeping them.

EDITH "EDIE" VONNEGUT is the eldest daughter of Kurt Vonnegut, Jr., and Jane Cox. She was born in Schenectady, New York, in 1949, and raised in Barnstable, Massachusetts. She works as a painter and has exhibited in galleries across the United States. She wrote and illustrated the book *Domestic Goddesses*. She has also served as a contributing illustrator to *The New York Times, Playboy,* and the Franklin Mint. She lives in the barn behind the house she grew up in, along with her husband, John Squibb, and has two sons and two grandchildren.

ABOUT THE TYPE

This book was set in Fournier, a typeface named for Pierre-Simon Fournier (1712–68), the youngest son of a French printing family. He started out engraving woodblocks and large capitals, then moved on to fonts of type. In 1736 he began his own foundry and made several important contributions in the field of type design; he is said to have cut 147 alphabets of his own creation. Fournier is probably best remembered as the designer of St. Augustine Ordinaire, a face that served as the model for the Monotype Corporation's Fournier, which was released in 1925.